NEW WINE INTERNATIONAL

THIRD DAY
PRAYERS

With

Joshua & Janet Angela Mills

NEW WINE INTERNATIONAL

NEW WINE INTERNATIONAL

THIRD DAY
PRAYERS

Joshua & Janet Angela Mills

ISBN: 978-0-578-05438-4

Published by **New Wine International, Inc.**
www.NewWineInternational.org

Special thanks and acknowledgment to Melanie Hart, for her labor of love in helping to compile this special prayer manual.

"Where There Is Great Love, There Are Always Great Miracles!"

Joshua & Janet Angela Mills

THIRD DAY PRAYERS

TABLE OF CONTENTS

INTRODUCTION..   12

    An Outline For Third Day Intercession......   13

    Twenty Tips For Intercessors................   17

    Protocol For Telephone Prayer Ministry....   23

    Protocol For Email Prayer Ministry...........   25

    How To Properly Pray For Others............   27

FAMILY

    Engagement..   30

    Marriage...   33

    Domestic Violence...............................   36

    Adultery..   39

    Sexual Sins..   42

    Abortion...   45

    Divorce..   48

    Restoration of Marriage.........................   51

FAMILY (CONTINUED)

Childbirth.. 54

Children.. 57

Rebellious Children............................... 60

HEALING

Physical Healing.................................. 64

Supernatural Weight-loss..................... 70

Age Renewal....................................... 75

Inner Healing...................................... 77

Emotional Healing............................... 82

Peaceful Sleep.................................... 85

FEAR

Worry... 90

Depression.. 93

Confusion.. 98

Discouragement.................................. 101

DELIVERANCE

Oppression.............................. 106

Demon Spirits........................... 109

Freedom from Addictions

Drugs.............................. 115

Alcohol............................ 118

Sexual............................. 121

Freedom from Disobedience............... 124

Freedom from Anger/Bitterness.............. 127

Freedom from Temptation.................... 130

Freedom from Complaining................... 133

Freedom from Guilt........................... 136

Freedom from the Occult..................... 139

Freedom from Suicide........................ 142

Breaking Generational Curses............... 146

Renewing the Mind........................... 149

Walking in Victory............................. 152

DESTINY

When All Looks Hopeless................... 156

The Will Of God................................ 159

Destiny Doors.................................. 162

FRUITFULNESS

Walking in Love................................ 166

Walking in Joy................................. 169

Walking in Peace.............................. 172

Walking in Patience........................... 175

Walking in Gentleness........................ 178

Walking in Goodness.......................... 181

Walking in Faithfulness....................... 184

Walking in Meekness.......................... 187

Walking in Self-Control....................... 190

SALVATION

Receiving Salvation............................ 194

Forgiveness.................................... 199

SALVATION (CONTINUED)

Unsaved Loved Ones........................... 202

HOLY SPIRIT & GLORY

Baptism in the Spirit............................. 206

Walking in the Glory Realm..................... 209

Faith.. 212

Visions & Dreams................................ 215

Empowerment.................................... 217

Anointing.. 220

Signs & Wonders................................ 223

Breaker Anointing............................... 225

Releasing Angels................................ 228

Open Heavens................................... 230

Impartation....................................... 232

LIFE ISSUES

A Nation And Its Leaders........................ 236

Attitude.. 239

LIFE ISSUES (CONTINUED)

Creativity.. 241

Desires... 243

Restoration Of Time.............................. 245

Romance.. 247

Losing A Loved One.............................. 249

Single Believer Desiring Marriage............. 252

Integrity.. 255

Wisdom.. 257

FINANCES

Daily Provision..................................... 260

Divine Cancellation Of Debt..................... 263

Employment.. 266

Tithes.. 269

Offerings.. 272

Seed.. 275

Multiplication Of Money........................... 278

Financial Pressure................................. 280

FINANCES (CONTINUED)

Financial Miracles................................... 283

THE CHURCH

The Local.. 286

Souls Harvest... 289

Revival in the Church............................... 291

PROMISES

Promises Of Answered Prayer.................... 296

Seven Promises Of God........................... 299

INTRODUCTION
BY
Joshua & Janet Angela Mills

We are so glad that you have chosen to use this Third Day Prayers manual and reference book!

After many years of ministry and long hours of studying the Word of God we have come to realize that the power of God is released as we choose to live by faith and walk in the Spirit of Glory!

We believe that this manual will give you these scriptural keys to release faith, anointing and glory in the midst of any situation. We have also included some brief practical training throughout the manual as a quick reference.

"The earnest (heartfelt, continued) prayer of a righteous man makes tremendous power available [dynamic in its working]."
– James 5:16

May this manual be both a blessing for your times of ministry, and a tremendous resource during your times of study.

In His Great Love,

Joshua & Janet Angela Mills

AN OUTLINE FOR THIRD DAY INTERCESSION

You should always use this following outline for your daily personal intercession (in preparation for your ministry assignments), as you begin actively declaring and releasing these statements over the following areas of your life:

- Home
- Family
- Church / Ministry
- Community
- Nation

GIVE... Give God all the glory in advance for what He is doing. Give Him praise and worship. Give of yourself to God through prayer and devotion. As you pray and intercede begin to write down your thoughts, feelings, words, visions, etc. This way you can give it to the body of Christ. It is good to write these things down and present it to your ministry leaders after your times of prayer. Give of your time and efforts through volunteering in a ministry position. Give financially to the ministry of New Wine International, and sow into the glory realm as the Lord gives you opportunity.

RELEASE... Release the people in the local area and around the world to come to the meetings, conferences, seminars and training schools. Release salvations. Release the captives to be set free. Release miracles, signs and wonders. Release revelation. Release finances. Release new sounds and heavenly worship. Release the Angelic host of heaven.

ANOINT... Anoint this ministry with the oil of the Holy Spirit as you pray and intercede. Anoint the ministry communications. Anoint the worship. Anoint the Word of God that will be spoken and declared. Anoint the ministry finances with the oil of protection and prosperity. Anoint Joshua & Janet Angela Mills and other ministry leaders. Anoint the offices, the office staff, the volunteers and all who participate in ministry functions. Anoint other Pastors and leadership team. Anoint the ministry of helps – the administration, the sound, the worship team, the workers and fellow laborers in the Harvest.

PRAY... Pray for Israel. Pray for your nation and the nations of the world. Pray for those in authority (Government and World Leaders). Keep Joshua & Janet Angela Mills and their family covered in prayer. Pray the blood of Jesus Christ over them, their home, their family, and every church/venue where they minister. Pray in the Spirit for those who will sit under this ministry – that they may have spiritual ears to hear, and eyes to see what the Holy Spirit is doing.

EXCEL... Excel in the glory realm. Let the Lord take you up into higher and new realms as you intercede. Watch your tongue. Avoid all gossip and careless talking, which will cause you to lose your focus (and it will bring you down). God is calling you UP in the things of the glory realm. You WILL excel in your intercession. Excel in the things of the Spirit – allow Him to take you to new places in your times of prayer and intercession.

GIVE!
RELEASE!
ANOINT!
PRAY!
EXCEL!

(See the diagram on next page)

THE NEW WINE
G.R.A.P.E.
AN OUTLINE FOR THIRD DAY INTERCESSION

Give   Luke 6:38

Release   Matthew 16:19

Anoint   Isaiah 10:27

Pray   1 Thessalonians 5:17

Excel   Jeremiah 29:11

TWENTY TIPS FOR INTERCESSORS

1. **Do Not Give Any Attention To The Enemy.** The devil is a defeated foe. We already have all the victory! The battle belongs to the Lord, but the blessing belongs to the children of God. Believe it and declare it!

2. **Do Not Over Spiritualize Everything.** Stay within biblical guidelines and stay operating in the Spirit of Truth. Every experience, every idea, every spiritual impression must be subject to the written Word of God. God will never say something contradictory to His Word.

3. **Do Not Get Into The Soulish Realm.** Do not allow the soul to dominate the Spirit. Do not minister out of hurts, feelings or emotions.

4. **Do Not Isolate Yourself** – join a recognized prayer ministry team and be surrounded by accountability to spiritual authority. Do not be a "Lone Ranger." Accountability will establish credibility!

17

5. **Do Not Partake In Manipulation**. We must always pray for "His will" to come to pass, not ours. Pray in partnership with God.

"This is the confidence we have in approaching God: that if we ask anything according to his will, he hears us. And if we know that he hears us—whatever we ask—we know that we have what we asked of him." (1 John 5:14-15)

6. **Do Not Participate In Flaky Activities.** God has called you to be "fruitful and multiply" – do not participate in activities that waste your precious time and produce no results. Stay fixed on God's Word and enter into the excellence of His glory!

7. **Pray From The Third Heaven.** Jesus only said what He heard His Father saying. Look unto the heavenlies and declare it on earth "as it is in heaven."

8. **Stay Close To The Heart Of God.** When you stay close to His heart you will always operate in a spirit of love and genuine compassion for others.

9. **Walk In Purity And Holiness.** Those who have "clean hands and a pure heart" will ascend the mountain of the Lord and stand in the glory. (Psalm 24)

10. **Guard Your Portals.** This includes the following gates: heart, eyes, ears, hands, feet and minds. Anoint them daily with the oil of the Holy Spirit.

11. **Praise Daily.** Your praise changes the atmosphere. It shakes nations, moves mountains, and opens prison doors. You don't praise because of what you're going through, you praise because of where you're going to! Your praise will move tomorrow's miracle into your NOW realm.

12. **Speak In The Now!** Change your vocabulary and begin speaking God's now revelation. God's Word is always fresh, living and active.

13. **Stay In The Spirit Of Worship.** Your worship will sustain the realm that your praise changes. The Spirit of worship is the key into the glory realm.

14. **Do Not Pray Within Your Limitations.** Pray in the Spirit and you will find yourself entering a dimension of God's limitless realm. This is the sphere where "all things are possible."

15. **Have An Attitude Of Gratitude.** Your thanksgiving unto God will open up doors of blessing. We enter into His gates with thanksgiving.

16. **Have A Miracle Mindset.** Believe for the miraculous. Renew your mind by putting on the mind of Christ. Take on His thoughts, His creativity, His ideas and His imagination.

    "Let this mind be in you, which was also in Christ Jesus." (Phil. 2:5 KJV)

17. **Seek "The New".** The bible says that "He is new every morning." There is always a new revelation and a new manifestation awaiting to be released through you!

18. **Enter Into The Ease Of The Glory.** Take time to rest in God's weighty glory cloud. Let the ease of His glory realm flow over you with life changing power.

19. **Live Within The Secret Place.** Every day seek to enter into a quiet place where there are no earthly distractions. Make your prayers known in that secret place, and listen for His voice. God will reward you openly.

20. **Stay In Your Rightful Position!** You are an Overcomer! You are Victorious! You are anointed of God and well able to receive the blessings of God's heavenly flow!

"...My house will be called a house of prayer for all nations."
– Isaiah 56:7

PROTOCOL FOR TELEPHONE PRAYER MINISTRY

Please use the following protocol when ministering in the telephone prayer ministry:

- Always work to create an atmosphere of love as defined by 1 Corinthians 13.

- Begin the call by saying... *"Praise the Lord, (insert your name) speaking, how may I pray with you today?"*

- Respect others by keeping your voice at a conversational level at all times while praying for others.

- Calls should be limited to approx. 3-5 minutes each

- You need to pray according to God's Word as outlined in the NWI Personal Ministry Prayer Manual.

PROTOCOL FOR TELEPHONE PRAYER MINISTRY
(Continued)

- Prayer will be a short prayer of agreement based upon God's promises and will not include any counsel or personal advice.

- Never release your personal contact information, email or phone number.

- Offer the caller recommended resources for further revelation in regards to their personal need(s). Refer to the NWI Ministry Resource Catalog.

- Always give an opportunity for the caller to sow into the ministry and outreach of New Wine International.

PROTOCOL FOR EMAIL/ONLINE PRAYER MINISTRY

Please use the following protocol when ministering in the email/online prayer ministry:

- Always remain in a spirit of love and atmosphere of glory as defined by 1 Corinthians 13.

- Begin all emails by stating... ***"Dear _____, Blessings in the name of Jesus Christ"***

- Emails should be limited to approximately four paragraphs each.
  - Opening
  - Prayer
  - Scriptures
  - Closing

- You will need to pray according to God's Word as outlined in the NWI Personal Ministry Prayer Manual.

PROTOCOL FOR EMAIL/ONLINE PRAYER MINISTRY (Continued)

- All email prayers will be a short prayer of agreement based upon God's promises and will not include any counsel or personal advice. You should always include at least two scripture verses within each email.

- Never release your personal contact information, email or phone number.

- Offer the caller recommended resources for further revelation in regards to their personal need(s). Refer to the NWI Ministry Resource Catalog.

- Always close each email by stating... *"In His Great Love, (Insert Your Name)"*

HOW TO PROPERLY PRAY FOR OTHERS

When you begin using this **Third Day Prayers** manual, you will begin to discover that we have included the Word of God along with each prayer.

You do not need to beg God and you do not need to plead with God. Through this manual we will teach you to simply "Thank God" for what He has already made available through the blood of Jesus Christ and the cross of Calvary. Once you thank Him, you can begin applying His Word to every situation you may encounter!

It is important to speak and declare the Word of God. It is the power that will set the captives free and release great restoration within many lives. I believe that the Holy Spirit has anointed you to pray for others, and this **Third Day Prayers** manual will help you to do just that!

The bible teaches us how to pray:

We pray to the Father, (Matt 6:9)
In the name of Jesus Christ, (John 14:14)
By the power of the Holy Spirit. (John 15:26)

NEW WINE INTERNATIONAL
MINISTRY NOTES

_____

_____

_____

_____

_____

_____

_____

_____

_____

_____

_____

_____

_____

_____

_____

_____

FAMILY

"By wisdom a house is built, and through understanding it is established."

Proverbs 24:3

ENGAGEMENT

SCRIPTURES
OLD TESTAMENT:

Ecclesiastes 4:12
Though one may be overpowered, two can defend themselves. A cord of three strands is not quickly broken.

Ezekiel 16:8
Later I passed by, and when I looked at you and saw that you were old enough for love, I spread the corner of My garment over you and covered your nakedness. I gave you My solemn oath and entered into a covenant with you, declares the Sovereign Lord, and you became Mine.

ENGAGEMENT

<u>SCRIPTURES</u>
NEW TESTAMENT:

Matthew 1:18

This is how the birth of Jesus Christ came about: His mother Mary was pledged to be married to Joseph, but before they came together, she was found to be with child through the Holy Spirit.

Luke 1:26-27

In the sixth month, God sent the angel Gabriel to Nazareth, a town in Galilee, to a virgin pledged to be married to a man named Joseph, a descendant of David. The virgin's name was Mary.

ENGAGEMENT

PRAYER

Father, I come to you in agreement for _____ and _____ as they prepare to share their life's Covenant with each other. I thank You for this precious couple, Lord. I know You have many exciting plans for their lives as they walk together and walk forward in unity. Help them to preserve this holy covenant as husband and wife and teach them to be one in the Spirit even now, Lord. Thank You that You have brought them together for such a time as this and I ask you to bring them closer to You in this preparation process as they submit their lives and their futures into Your hands. Teach them that through their honesty, trust and undivided agreement You will always be surrounding them with Your matchless wisdom and love as they call upon You in times of need. Fill their hearts with Your peace now which removes any fear, anxiety or concern. May they be continually filled with Your Spirit, Lord, as they make one of the most important commitments of their lives, in Jesus' Name, Amen.

MARRIAGE

SCRIPTURES
OLD TESTAMENT:

Ezekiel 37:26
I will make a covenant of peace with them; it will be an everlasting covenant. I will establish them and increase their numbers, and I will put My sanctuary among them forever.

Jeremiah 29:6
Marry and have sons and daughters; find wives for your sons and give your daughters in marriage, so that they too may have sons and daughters. Increase in number there; do not decrease.

MARRIAGE

<u>SCRIPTURES</u>
NEW TESTAMENT:

Colossians 3:18
Wives, submit to your husbands, as is fitting in the Lord.

Ephesians 5:23
The husband is the head of the wife as Christ is the head of the Church, His body, of which He is the Savior.

<u>Other Scriptures:</u>
Hebrews 13:4
Genesis 2:18,24
Mark 10:6-9
Ephesians 5:31-33

MARRIAGE

PRAYER

Heavenly Father, in the mighty Name above all Names, I lift up the marriage of _____ and _____. Bless this marriage, Lord, bring an increase of awareness in their hearts and minds of the mighty plans You have for this marriage. Help them now in the areas that they may be struggling with, by the power of Your Spirit. Let there be unity, commitment and agreement like never before. Increase their hunger to study Your Word and pray together. Keep them far from any unforgiveness or bitterness that may have tried to creep in to their union. Cleanse them now from any thoughts, words or actions that may have tried to divide. Let them know that their agreement together as a couple is vital in this hour and help them to pursue harmony and unity. Assign and send ministering angels to protect and strengthen this union, Lord. We trust You with their lives and we commit them into Your hands to be used mightily as an example of unity, righteousness and power for Your Glory. Let their lives be a testimony and example that lifts up and glorifies Your Name, in Jesus' mighty Name, Amen.

DOMESTIC VIOLENCE

<u>SCRIPTURES</u>
OLD TESTAMENT:

Psalms 55:1-3

Listen to my prayer, O God, do not ignore my plea; hear me and answer me. My thoughts trouble me and I am distraught at the voice of the enemy, at the stares of the wicked; for they bring down suffering upon me and revile me in their anger.

Job 1:10

Have You not put a hedge around him and his household and everything he has? You have blessed the work of his hands, so that his flocks and herds are spread throughout the land.

DOMESTIC VIOLENCE

<u>SCRIPTURES</u>
NEW TESTAMENT:

Luke 6:28
Bless those who curse you, pray for those who mistreat you.

Luke 21:18
But not a hair of your head will perish.

Luke 10:6
If a man of peace is there, your peace will rest on him; if not, it will return to you.

NEW WINE INTERNATIONAL

DOMESTIC VIOLENCE

<u>PRAYER</u>

Dear Lord Jesus, we thank You for Your protective covering that is surrounding _____ right now. I ask you to give him/her Your supernatural wisdom, direction and comfort by the Spirit. Thank You that Your shield of faith quenches all the fiery darts of their enemies. I ask for Divine angelic intervention in both their lives, Lord. I speak healing to the broken hearts, healing to the broken spirits, healing to the wounds that have been inflicted right now in Jesus' mighty Name. I ask for a miracle where it is needed, Lord. I call upon heavenly hosts to release the captives now, Lord, declaring deliverance according to Your will, Father. May _____ and _____ learn to fear and trust You like never before. Bless them with an awareness of Your presence and I thank You that You are always present when _____ calls upon You, Lord. You are faithful to heal, deliver and carry their burdens. We worship You for Your Divine intervention today, Lord. Thank You for the turnaround, the breakthrough in the Spirit, that will be seen by many. We glorify You in that matchless Name of Jesus, Amen.

ADULTERY

SCRIPTURES
OLD TESTAMENT:

Deuteronomy 5:18
You shall not commit adultery.

Proverbs 6:32
But a man who commits adultery lacks judgment; whoever does so destroys himself.

ADULTERY

SCRIPTURES
NEW TESTAMENT:

Mark 10:19
You know the commandments: do not murder, do not commit adultery, do not steal, do not give false testimony, do not defraud, honor your father and mother.

John 8:4, 7-11
They said to Jesus, Teacher, this woman was caught in the act of adultery. When they kept on questioning Him, He straightened up and said to them, If any one of you is without sin, let him be the first to throw a stone at her. Again He stooped down and wrote on the ground. At this, those who heard began to go away one at a time, the older ones first, until only Jesus was left, with the woman still standing there. Jesus straightened up and asked her, Woman, where are they? Has no one condemned you? No one, sir, she said. Then neither do I condemn you, Jesus declared. Go now and leave your life of sin.

ADULTERY

<u>PRAYER</u>

Heavenly Father, thank You for the precious gift of the Covenant of marriage. I come to You on behalf of _____ and _____ during this time of attack and division in their marriage. I ask You to intervene in _____'s life, and remind he/she that Your will is agreement, holiness and purity. Release a conviction of repentance now, in Jesus' mighty Name. I ask for healing in the hearts of _____ and _____. Begin to bring restoration to this marriage, Lord, through Your mercy, Divine healing and forgiveness. Pour out Your unconditional love on them both, Lord and remove and dismiss and renounce all critical words that have been thought or spoken. Remove all guilt, condemnation and unworthiness from their hearts and minds. Give them hearts of flesh and remove the stony places that kept _____ bound in fulfilling the desires of the flesh instead of the Spirit. I speak freedom to them, as You began the healing and restoration today. You are faithful and Your mercies are new every morning. We put our trust in Your Word that heals because everything is possible with You, in the mighty Name of Jesus, Amen.

SEXUAL SINS

<u>SCRIPTURES</u>
OLD TESTAMENT:

Leviticus 18:20

Do not have sexual relations with your neighbor's wife and defile yourself with her.

Genesis 4:7

If you do what is right, will you not be accepted? But if you do not do what is right, sin is crouching at your door; it desires to have you, but you must master it."

SEXUAL SINS

SCRIPTURES
NEW TESTAMENT:

Galatians 5:19-21
The acts of the sinful nature are obvious: sexual immorality, impurity and debauchery; idolatry and witchcraft; hatred, discord, jealousy, fits of rage, selfish ambition, dissensions, factions and envy; drunkenness, orgies, and the like. I warn you, as I did before, that those who live like this will not inherit the Kingdom of God.

Romans 12:1-2
Therefore, I urge you, brothers, in view of God's mercy, to offer your bodies as living sacrifices, holy and pleasing to God—this is your spiritual act of worship.

SEXUAL SINS

<ins>PRAYER</ins>

Father, I thank You for Your holiness, Your righteousness that is being poured out on _____ even right now. Thank You that You are cancelling the assignment on this life by Your blood and releasing Your Holy Spirit and a host of angels to deliver and heal, Lord. Your plan and purpose for him/her is great and I thank You for the fulfillment of holy dreams and desires that glorify You. Let the desire for the flesh begin to diminish now as Your power and spiritual authority through the Blood of Jesus intervenes for this life. Thank You for turnaround, Father; this life will bring glory and honor to Your Name and be a powerful witness that will minister to others. We expect and receive a miracle breakthrough for _____ and a lifestyle pleasing to You. I ask You to remove all the wrong people from this life and bring in those specific people who will encourage, be an example and love him/her unconditionally. I decree a love for the Word to spring forth, washing _____ and making him/her clean and new. Thank You for a new heart, Lord and we ask this in the powerful Name of Jesus, Amen.

ABORTION

<u>SCRIPTURES</u>
OLD TESTAMENT:

Psalms 3:3
But you are a shield around me, O Lord; You bestow glory on me and lift up my head.

Ezekiel 36:25
I will sprinkle clean water on you, and you will be clean; I will cleanse you from all your impurities and from all your idols.

ABORTION

<u>SCRIPTURES</u>
NEW TESTAMENT:

Revelation 12:10-12
Then I heard a loud voice in heaven say: "Now have come the salvation and the power and the Kingdom of our God, and the authority of His Christ. For the accuser of our brothers, who accuses them before our God day and night, has been hurled down. They overcame him by the blood of the Lamb and by the word of their testimony; they did not love their lives so much as to shrink from death.

Galatians 6:1
Brothers, if someone is caught in a sin, you who are spiritual should restore him gently. But watch yourself, or you also may be tempted.

ABORTION

<u>PRAYER</u>

Jesus, we lift up _____ to You right now. Intervene mightily in this situation, whether she is contemplating an abortion or has had one. I ask for complete renewing of her mind, Lord. We pray in agreement that there will be immediate release of all guilt, condemnation or unforgiveness and an immediate honor for life, Lord. We decree this baby will live and not die, that its little life is precious to You, Jesus. Release Your wisdom, Your peace, Your protection now, in Jesus' Name. I ask for complete and total surrender to Your will, with humility and trust that You will guide and provide for _____ and her baby. I declare her decisions will line up with Your Word and I cancel the assignment of death and guilt by the power of Jesus Christ against _____. I decree complete freedom in her mind and heart as she commits her life to you, a fresh and a new. Let this miracle turnaround bring You glory and honor as You work wonders on her behalf. Impart Your peace now and give her Your love. Thank You for the great love You have for her and her baby. In Jesus mighty Name we pray, Amen.

DIVORCE

SCRIPTURES
OLD TESTAMENT:

Jeremiah 30:17
But I will restore you to health and heal your wounds, declares the Lord, because you are called an outcast, Zion for whom no one cares.

Malachi 2:14
You ask, "Why?" It is because the Lord is acting as the witness between you and the wife of your youth, because you have broken faith with her, though she is your partner, the wife of your marriage covenant.

DIVORCE

<u>SCRIPTURES</u>
NEW TESTAMENT:

1 Peter 5:10
And the God of all grace, who called you to His eternal glory in Christ, after you have suffered a little while, will Himself restore you and make you strong, firm and steadfast.

Matthew 19:3-8
They asked, Is it lawful for a man to divorce his wife for any and every reason? Haven't you read, he replied, that at the beginning the Creator made them male and female, and said, For this reason a man will leave his father and mother and be united to his wife, and the two will become one flesh? So they are no longer two, but one. Therefore what God has joined together, let man not separate. Why then, they asked, did Moses command that a man give his wife a certificate of divorce and send her away?" Jesus replied, Moses permitted you to divorce your wives because your hearts were hard. But it was not this way from the beginning.

DIVORCE

<u>PRAYER</u>

Dear Lord, I lift up _____ to You and thank You for his/her life and destiny. I pray for healing of the emotions, healing of his/her heart, and healing of the wounds of disappointment and rejection, right now in Jesus' mighty Name. I thank You for Your forgiveness and unconditional love and ask You to give them a sense of great worth because of the blood of Jesus. Thank You for providing supernaturally in the area of finances and friendships. We praise You for giving him/her a future that is bright with Your presence and hope. I pray for a heart to forgive the spouse and healing for any children or others who may be involved, nothing missing, nothing broken, Lord. Remove the stain of guilt or condemnation from any words that may have been spoken that did not line up with Your Word and declare they are cancelled in Jesus' Name. In times of great loneliness let Your presence and Your glory surround them and give them peace. I thank You for _____ and the love You have for him/her. We pray in agreement for new life & new hope to spring forth now, in Jesus' Name, Amen.

RESTORATION OF MARRIAGE

<u>SCRIPTURES</u>
OLD TESTAMENT:

Hosea 3:1
The Lord said to me, Go, show your love to your wife again, though she is loved by another and is an adulteress. Love her as the Lord loves the Israelites, though they turn to other gods and love the sacred raisin cakes.

Nehemiah 1:8
Remember the instruction you gave your servant Moses, saying, If you are unfaithful, I will scatter you among the nations, but if you return to Me and obey My commands, then even if your exiled people are at the farthest horizon, I will gather them from there and bring them to the place I have chosen as a dwelling for My Name.

RESTORATION
OF
MARRIAGE

SCRIPTURES
NEW TESTAMENT:

Matthew 17:11
Jesus replied, To be sure, Elijah comes and will restore all things.

1 Peter 5:10
And the God of all grace, who called you to His eternal glory in Christ, after you have suffered a little while, will Himself restore you and make you strong, firm and steadfast.

RESTORATION OF MARRIAGE

PRAYER

Lord Jesus, _____ and I pray in agreement right now for the restoration of this marriage. I thank You for a miracle, Lord. I thank You that nothing is too hard for you, so we can expect that You hear us when we pray. We ask for a change in hearts, a change in mindsets, a change in direction for everyone involved in this Covenant. I ask You to work humility and unconditional love in the hearts of _____ and _____, Lord. May they be drawn closer to You and closer to each other during this time. Free them from any bitterness or judging. Change the atmosphere in their home, Father, to be full of peace and tranquility and that they would recognize that it is Your presence. I pray that this marriage be founded on the rock of Your Word and that obedience and fear of God will spring forth. Pour out Your glory on this union and bring it back together as You revive the hearts of _____ and _____. Let there be revival in this family, Lord. We thank You and praise You, Amen.

CHILDBIRTH

<u>SCRIPTURES</u>
OLD TESTAMENT

Ecclesiastes 11:10
So then, banish anxiety from your heart and cast off the troubles of your body, for youth and vigor are meaningless.

Jeremiah 31:8
See, I will bring them from the land of the north and gather them from the ends of the earth. Among them will be the blind and the lame, expectant mothers and women in labor; a great throng will return.

1 Chronicles 4:10
Jabez cried out to the God of Israel, Oh, that You would bless me and enlarge my territory! Let Your hand be with me, and keep me from harm so that I will be free from pain. And God granted his request.

CHILDBIRTH

SCRIPTURES
NEW TESTAMENT

John 16:21
A woman giving birth to a child has pain because her time has come; but when her baby is born she forgets the anguish because of her joy that a child is born into the world.

1Timothy 2:15
But women will be saved through childbearing--if they continue in faith, love and holiness with propriety.

CHILDBIRTH

<u>PRAYER</u>

I thank You, Father, that You are covering this womb with Your sweet love. I pray for _____ right now that she will be aware of Your presence as You help her bring forth this precious life. I ask You for a quick and pain-free delivery and supernatural peace in the delivery room. Even now go before _____ and prepare the room with angels and a cloud of Your glory that ushers in this new life. Release health and vitality to mother and baby and prepare and guide the doctors and nurses with Your hand. Let there be great provision for this little one, supernatural protection, finances, wisdom and a love for Your Word. Surround this baby with family and friends who will nurture him/her with a great love for You, Father. I cancel any assignment of fear or worry off this precious mother right now and I ask You to help her in this wonderful new beginning. Bless this union of mother, father and baby and let nothing come to divide them. Strengthen _____ for the task that is set before her and give her peace. We dedicate this family to You, Lord. In Jesus' mighty Name, Amen.

CHILDREN

SCRIPTURES
OLD TESTAMENT

Psalms 127:3
Sons are a heritage from the Lord, children a reward from Him.

Proverbs 22:6
Train up a child in the way he should go, and when he is old he will not turn from it.

Isaiah 54:13
All your sons will be taught by the Lord and great will be your children's peace.

CHILDREN

SCRIPTURES
NEW TESTAMENT

Ephesians 6:1-3
Children, obey your parents in the Lord, for this is right. Honor your father and mother which is the first commandment with a promise, that it may go well with you and that you may enjoy long life on the earth.

Colossians 3:21
Fathers, do not embitter your children, or they will become discouraged.

CHILDREN

PRAYER

Lord, parenting a child is a sacred privilege so we come before You to lift up _____ to You right now and ask that You fill them with Divine heavenly blessings, encounters and more of Your presence, Lord. I pray for the Holy Spirit to be poured out on him/her that they may prophesy and see visions and bring glory to Your Name. Your faithful love and power will enable them to lead lives pleasing to You. We declare this child is free from abuse, free from harmful words that may have been spoken. We cancel any assignment that is not of God and we declare this child will fulfill the call on his/her life and walk in the destiny that has been planned before the foundation of the earth. I pray for the parents that they would be filled with wisdom and knowledge in parenting this child. Teach them how to respond and not react, how to care and not control. I stand in agreement for _____ that his/her gifts and callings would be recognized and he/she will walk in that calling with You, Lord. I pray for safety, for angels to protect them as grow and learn and be everything You have called them to be. In Jesus' Name, Amen.

REBELLIOUS CHILDREN

<u>SCRIPTURES</u>
OLD TESTAMENT

Malachi 4:6
He will turn the hearts of the fathers to their children, and the hearts of the children to their fathers; or else I will come and strike the land with a curse.

Deuteronomy 30:19
This day I call heaven and earth as witnesses against you that I have set before you life and death, blessings and curses. Now choose life, so that you and your children may live.

REBELLIOUS CHILDREN

SCRIPTURES
NEW TESTAMENT

Luke 15:8-10
Or suppose a woman has ten silver coins and loses one. Does she not light a lamp, sweep the house and search carefully until she finds it? And when she finds it, she calls her friends and neighbors together and says, Rejoice with me; I have found my lost coin. In the same way, I tell you, there is rejoicing in the presence of the angels of God over one sinner who repents.

Romans 8:28
And we know that in all things God works for the good of those who love Him, who have been called according to His purpose.

Acts 16:31
They replied, Believe in the Lord Jesus, and you will be saved--you and your household.

REBELLIOUS CHILDREN

PRAYER

Dear heavenly Father, we lift up (child's name) to You right now and thank You for Your love for them. We know You have a plan and a purpose for good and not for evil so we declare that they will fulfill that call and that plan. We decree that _____ will turn from their imperfect ways and submit to Your perfect ways. I thank You for intervening in their life right now, that You change a heart of rebellion into a heart of obedience. Wherever they are I ask You to renew their mind with the power of the Holy Spirit and the Word of God. Open their eyes to the Truth that they would recognize the deception they are living in. Close the doors to wrong relationships and open the doors to new friends who know You. Deliver them from evil and bring them into Your glorious freedom that is waiting for them. Let them feel Your glorious love as You wrap Your loving arms around them right now. Bless them with peace and if they are away from home I ask that You protect them and lead them unto the path of life. We thank You for miracles and signs and wonders for this child, Lord. In Jesus' Name, Amen.

HEALING

"Praise the Lord, O my soul, and forget not all his
benefits - who forgives all your sins and heals all
your diseases."
Psalm 103:2-3

PHYSICAL HEALING

FACTS:

SICKNESS IS A SPIRIT:

The Word of God makes it clear that sickness and disease is a spirit. Look at the biblical examples found in the following passages of scripture:

- Luke 13:10-16
- Matthew 17:15-18

Whenever you are ministering physical healing to a person, you will need to command the specific spirit of sickness (example: spirit of the flu, spirit of migraines, etc.) to leave the person's body.

The bible says that you can take authority over these spirits of sickness and disease. Through salvation in Jesus Christ, God has given you the power to set the captives free!

Jesus said *"I have given you authority to trample on snakes and scorpions and to overcome all the power of the enemy; nothing will harm you."* (Luke 10:19)

PHYSICAL HEALING

<u>FACTS:</u>

<u>SPEAK THE WORD OF GOD:</u>

Proverbs 4:20-22
"My son, pay attention to what I say; listen closely to my words. Do not let them out of your sight, keep them within your heart; for they are life to those who find them and health to a man's whole body."
The Hebrew word for "health" in this passage of scripture is "medicine." This scripture says that God's Word is medicine to our whole body!

Jesus said "…The words I have spoken to you are spirit and they are life." (John 6:63)

God's Words are spirit and they are life![1]

---

[1] When speaking the Word of God for healing, you may want to refer to the "Healing For Your Body" Ministry Card. This is available through the ministry and pertains to specific areas of the physical body.

PHYSICAL HEALING

<u>HOW TO MINISTER:</u>

Always remember to pray in the following way:

- ➤ To the Father
- ➤ In the name of Jesus Christ
- ➤ By the power of the Holy Spirit

When you prepare to minister physical healing to someone remember this simple guideline:

1. Command the spirit of sickness (give a specific name to it, example: spirit of cancer, spirit of diabetes, etc.) to leave the person's body.

2. Command the body to be made whole. Once again speaking to the specific body part (example: I command your liver to be made whole in the name of Jesus Christ).

3. Speak the Word of God over the situation. Give a few healing scriptures to the one you're ministering to – as God's Word is Spirit and life!

PHYSICAL HEALING

<u>SCRIPTURES</u>
OLD TESTAMENT:

Exodus 23:25
Worship the Lord your God, and his blessing will be on your food and water. I will take away sickness from among you.

Psalms 107:20
He sent forth His Word and healed them; He rescued them from the grave.

Isaiah 58:8
Then your light will break forth like the dawn, and your healing will quickly appear; then your righteousness will go before you, and the glory of the Lord will be your rear guard.

PHYSICAL HEALING

SCRIPTURES
NEW TESTAMENT:

Matthew 9:20-22
Just then a woman who had been subject to bleeding for twelve years came up behind Him and touched the edge of His cloak. She said to herself, If I only touch His cloak, I will be healed. Jesus turned and saw her. Take heart, daughter, He said, your faith has healed you. And the woman was healed from that moment.

Matthew 4:23
Jesus went throughout Galilee, teaching in their synagogues, preaching the good news of the kingdom, and healing every disease and sickness among the people.

Matthew 14:14
When Jesus landed and saw a large crowd, He had compassion on them and healed their sick.

PHYSICAL HEALING

<u>PRAYER</u>

Lord of glory, You are the Great Physician and all healing comes from Your mighty hands. I stand in agreement with _____ for complete and total healing right now in Jesus' mighty Name. You took his/her infirmities, carried their sicknesses and cancelled their diseases by willingly shedding Your blood on the cross for them. Since we know it is Your will they be healed we rebuke and renounce the spirit of infirmity. We put our trust in Your matchless Word as You send Your Word to appropriate that healing. You said the prayer of faith will heal the sick so we stand together in faith now for _____ that they are healed in Jesus' Name. Thank You for Your compassion on their situation and their struggles; deliver them now from all that oppresses them physically. You promised to cause their health to be restored and spring forth speedily and heal all their wounds. We believe You, Father and thank You right now for all that You've done and all You are doing. We declare physical and emotional freedom for _____ right now. We praise You, Lord; in Jesus' Name, Amen.

SUPERNATURAL WEIGHT-LOSS

FACTS:

STATISTICS:

- Percent of adults age 20 years and over who are overweight or obese: 67% (2005-2006)
- Percent of adolescents age 12-19 years who are overweight: 18% (2005-2006)
- Percent of children age 6-11 years who are overweight: 15% (2005-2006)
- Percent of children age 2-5 years who are overweight: 11% (2005-2006) [2]

REASONS FOR OBESITY:

- Lack of exercise or physical activity
- Wrong food choices (fast food, etc.)
- Stress or daily pressures
- Abuse or some other traumatic event(s)
- Overeating or a spirit of gluttony
- Spirit of infirmity (disease or other sickness)

---

[2] Information received from Centers For Disease Control and Prevention

SUPERNATURAL WEIGHT-LOSS

<u>HOW TO MINISTER:</u>

Obesity has become a major problem within our society – but God has the answer to this problem!

When beginning to minister supernatural weight-loss to someone, you will need to determine the cause of the excess weight.

<u>SOME EXAMPLES:</u>

- If the person is making the wrong food choices, you will need to pray for a spirit of wisdom.

- If the person is overeating, you will need to command the spirit of gluttony to leave.

- If abuse or some other traumatic event is involved, you may need to deal with issues of unforgiveness.

SUPERNATURAL WEIGHT-LOSS

SCRIPTURES
OLD TESTAMENT:

Psalm 107:9
For He satisfies the thirsty and fills the hungry with good things.

Proverbs 3:5
Trust in the Lord with all your heart and lean not on your own understanding.

Isaiah 40:31
But those who hope in the Lord will renew their strength. They will soar on wings like eagles; they will run and not grow weary, they will walk and not be faint.

SUPERNATURAL WEIGHT-LOSS

SCRIPTURES
NEW TESTAMENT:

Romans 14:17
For the kingdom of God is not a matter of eating and drinking, but of righteousness, peace and joy in the Holy Spirit.

1 Corinthians 10:31
So whether you eat or drink or whatever you do, do it all for the glory of God.

Hebrews 12:1
Wherefore seeing we also are compassed about with so great a cloud of witnesses, let us lay aside every weight, and the sin which doth so easily beset us, and let us run with patience the race that is set before us.

Other Scriptures:
Psalm 16:7
Philippians 4:13
2 Corinthians 5:17
Hebrews 12:11

SUPERNATURAL WEIGHT-LOSS

PRAYER

Father, in the name of Jesus Christ, I thank you for releasing supernatural weight-loss on _____ by the power of Your Holy Spirit.

In the name of Jesus, I speak to your body and I curse the cells, roots, seeds and branches of excess weight. I take authority and dominion and I command you "spirit of heaviness" to come out now! I rebuke this excess weight, and I command a supernatural weight-loss from the realms of glory. I command any spirit of disbelief and unbelief to come out now as well!

I command all spirits of infirmity to come out now, and I rebuke any and all medical conditions associated with this temporary extra weight. I reverse any spirit of inheritance or generational curse of being overweight. I command the appestat to return to its proper balance and harmony, and for it to function with perfection as God intended it to. Thank you, Lord, for the new slim and trim weight to begin manifesting in the name of Jesus Christ.

AGE RENEWAL

<u>SCRIPTURES</u>
OLD TESTAMENT:

Psalm 21:4
He asked you for life, and you gave it to him - length of days, forever and ever.

Psalm 103:1,5
Praise the Lord, O my soul... who satisfies your desires with good things so that your youth is renewed like the eagle's.

Exodus 23:25-26
Worship the Lord your God, and his blessing will be on your food and water. I will take away sickness from among you... I will give you a full life span.

Deuteronomy 34:7
Moses was a hundred and twenty years old when he died, yet his eyes were not weak nor his strength gone.

AGE RENEWAL

<u>SCRIPTURES</u>
NEW TESTAMENT:

James 5:15
And the prayer offered in faith will make the sick person well; the Lord will raise him up. If he has sinned, he will be forgiven.

1 Peter 3:10,11
Whoever would love life and see good days must keep his tongue from evil... He must turn from evil and do good; he must seek peace and pursue it.

3 John 1:2
I pray that you may enjoy good health and that all may go well with you, even as your soul is getting along well.

INNER HEALING

FACTS

Inner healing is a ministry that seeks to deal with inner pain (both emotional and spiritual). This inner pain may be present due to negative life experiences. An example of this is someone who was badly treated by one or both parents during childhood. They may have been sexually abused or perhaps just generally ignored - not properly valued and loved. If someone suffered rejection in childhood, there may still be evidence of this in the person's life. Perhaps that person may find it difficult to love others, or perhaps they may experience depression or a negative life attitude due to the damage.

When a person has been deeply hurt within, it affects not only their emotions but also their inner spirit. If an individual is hurt repeatedly over an extended period of time their spirit will often become weak and broken.

"A man's spirit sustains him in sickness, but a crushed spirit who can bear?"
– Proverbs 18:14

INNER HEALING

HOW TO MINISTER

Generally in order to receive inner healing it will be imperative for the person to release all feelings of anger, bitterness, resentment, self-pity and unforgiveness.

When ministering to this person, you will need to ask the Lord to reveal underlying issues and situations in order to minister effectively so that the person may receive complete freedom and healing.

HOW TO PRAY WITH A PERSON TO RECEIVE INNER HEALING

Ask the person to do the following:

1. Recognize the areas where they have become wounded in their spirit.

2. Allow God to heal them and their wounds.

3. Guard their spirit against becoming wounded.

INNER HEALING

SCRIPTURES
OLD TESTAMENT

Ezekiel 11:19
I will give them an undivided heart and put a new spirit in them; I will remove from them their heart of stone and give them a heart of flesh.

Hosea 14:4-5
I will heal their waywardness and love them freely, for My anger has turned away from them. I will be like the dew to Israel; he will blossom like a lily. Like a cedar of Lebanon he will send down his roots.

Exodus 15:26
He said, If you listen carefully to the voice of the Lord your God and do what is right in His eyes, if you pay attention to His commands and keep all His decrees, I will not bring on you any of the diseases I brought on the Egyptians, for I am the Lord, who heals you.

INNER HEALING

<u>SCRIPTURES</u>
NEW TESTAMENT

Romans 12:2
Do not conform any longer to the pattern of this world, but be transformed by the renewing of your mind. Then you will be able to test and approve what God's will is— His good, pleasing and perfect will.

2 Corinthians 10:5
We demolish arguments and every pretension that sets itself up against the knowledge of God, and we take captive every thought to make it obedient to Christ.

Matthew 9:36
When He saw the crowds, He had compassion on them, because they were harassed and helpless, like sheep without a shepherd.

INNER HEALING

<u>PRAYER</u>

Dear Lord Jesus, thank You for Your great love and compassion for the hurting. I come to You now, in the Name of Jesus on behalf of _____. Nothing can separate him/her from Your matchless love. You have delivered him/her from the power of darkness and have translated them into Your Kingdom. I ask You to remove their heart of stone and replace it with a heart of flesh, where Your new covenant of love is written. Replace the memories and words that have bruised them with new thoughts of power and love and soundness of mind. We take captive every thought and every deep wound and make it obedient to Christ. In Jesus' Name we agree for complete healing to their mind, their heart and their emotions. Holy Spirit, You are the great Comforter and their ever present help in time of need. We ask for complete forgiveness, for themselves and for others who have hurt them. Let no bitter root of offense remain and we know the power of God has gone forth now and begun this mighty work. In Jesus' mighty Name, Amen.

EMOTIONAL HEALING

SCRIPTURES
OLD TESTAMENT

Psalms 41:3
The Lord will sustain him on his sickbed and restore him from his bed of illness.

Isaiah 57:18
I have seen his ways, but I will heal him; I will guide him and restore comfort to him.

Jeremiah 30:17
But I will restore you to health and heal your wounds, declares the Lord, because you are called an outcast, Zion for whom no one cares.

EMOTIONAL HEALING

<u>SCRIPTURES</u>
NEW TESTAMENT

Luke 9:11
He welcomed them and spoke to them about the Kingdom of God, and healed those who needed healing.

2 Thessalonians 1:7
And give relief to you who are troubled, and to us as well. This will happen when the Lord Jesus is revealed from heaven in blazing fire with His powerful angels.

EMOTIONAL HEALING

<u>PRAYER</u>

Lord Jesus, You understand the feelings of betrayal, persecution and rejection. Because of Your great love for _____, we come to You in agreement for Your overcoming power of healing to his/her emotions. We pray for those who inflicted the deep hurts, pray for their healing and freedom from guilt. You bore our grief and carried our sorrows so we can thank You for lifting the burden of pain and memories from _____. Nothing is too difficult for You, Lord, so we anticipate new emotions, new joy, new freedom as You appropriate the healing power of Jesus to him/her right now. Remove the fear, canceling the words that have been spoken against him/her. Help him/her to walk in love, hungering for Your Word and releasing forgiveness to those who have wronged him/her. I declare it is a new day for _____. I decree hope and wholeness to him/her right now in Jesus' mighty Name. I command destiny and revelations to come forth! Healing come forth! We thank You by faith that it is done because of Jesus' great love, Amen.

PEACEFUL SLEEP

<u>SCRIPTURES</u>
OLD TESTAMENT

Psalms 4:7-8
You have filled my heart with greater joy than when their grain and new wine abound. I will lie down and sleep in peace, for You alone, O Lord, make me dwell in safety.

Proverbs 3:24
When you lie down, you will not be afraid; when you lie down, your sleep will be sweet.

Jeremiah 31:25-26
I will refresh the weary and satisfy the faint. At this I awoke and looked around. My sleep had been pleasant to me.

PEACEFUL SLEEP

<u>SCRIPTURES</u>
NEW TESTAMENT

Matthew 11:28
Come to Me, all you who are weary and burdened, and I will give you rest.

Hebrews 4:3
Now we who have believed enter that rest, just as God has said.

PEACEFUL SLEEP

<u>PRAYER</u>

Father, thank You for the precious gift of peaceful sleep You are bestowing on _____ right now. Remove any anxiety, worry, cares or fear that does not belong to them. We cast them all at Your feet, by faith. When they lie down they will not be afraid, but their sleep will be sweet because they trust completely in You, Lord. You give Your beloved sleep, Lord, and we believe Your Word is true and forever settled in heaven. May this be the beginning of a new walk of trust, a new walk of faith and agreement with Your Word for _____. Help him/her to remember that when trouble or anxiety tries to come, or when circumstances seem to close in on them they will cast all their cares on You and worship You in the midst of these storms. You are the answer, the door, the wisdom, the hope and the light unto their path. You will refresh the weary and satisfy the faint with peaceful sleep. We decree that for _____ right now and expect a change because precious Holy Spirit is there right now bringing Comfort and Peace. Thank You precious Lord, in Jesus' Name we pray, Amen.

NEW WINE INTERNATIONAL
HEALING NOTES

FEAR

"There is no fear in love. But perfect love drives out fear, because fear has to do with punishment. The one who fears is not made perfect in love."

1 John 4:18

WORRY

SCRIPTURES
OLD TESTAMENT:

Psalms 34:4
I sought the Lord, and He answered me; He delivered me from all my fears.

Psalms 37:8
Refrain from anger and turn from wrath; do not fret—it leads only to evil.

WORRY

<u>SCRIPTURES</u>
NEW TESTAMENT:

Matthew 6:34
Therefore do not worry about tomorrow, for tomorrow will worry about itself. Each day has enough trouble of its own.

Philippians 4:6
Do not be anxious about anything, but in everything, by prayer and petition, with thanksgiving, present your requests to God.

John 14:27
Peace I leave with you; My peace I give you. I do not give to you as the world gives. Do not let your hearts be troubled and do not be afraid.

WORRY

<u>PRAYER</u>

Father, You said in Your Word to be anxious for nothing, but in everything, by prayer and petition, with thanksgiving, present our requests to You. So I stand in agreement right now with _____ presenting his/her cares to You for complete removal of any worry, fear or anxiety. Holy Spirit, bring Your peace to him/her, filling them with comfort and rest. I declare freedom from the worry, freedom to their mind, freedom from anxiety in Jesus' Name. He/she will not be afraid because his/her heart and mind is fixed on You, Father. Help him/her to grow in his/her ability to trust You, and cause true joy and blessing to come to them now as they trust in You with all their heart. I declare these situations that have caused them to worry be resolved in Jesus' Name. Holy Spirit bring comfort, peace and wisdom right now as You cause these situations to dissolve and faith and trust explode in their life. Teach him/her to keep his/her eyes to be fixed on You and Your Word, Lord. Thank You for Your wonderful faithfulness, Jesus; there is none like You. In Jesus' Name we expect a blanket of peace now for _____, Amen.

DEPRESSION

FACTS

- Depression is considered a major illness affecting millions of people at various stages of life.

- It is a demon spirit that Satan uses to attack the mind, thoughts and emotions of a person.

- It is not only a major mental problem, but it is also recognized as a serious health threat which often triggers major problems affecting the spiritual, mental and physical body of a person.

- Depression often opens a door towards suicidal thoughts. (see **Suicide** pg.138)

Thought patterns must be changed. As long as a person allows thoughts of worry, defeat or depression to remain, they will be depressed.

"For as he thinketh in his heart, so is he."
– Prov. 23:7 (KJV)

God has an answer for depression – it is the Word of God! Because the Word says that we are victorious! We need to think on His Word!

DEPRESSION

<u>SCRIPTURES</u>
OLD TESTAMENT:

Psalms 43:5
Why are you downcast, O my soul? Why so disturbed within me? Put your hope in God, for I will yet praise Him, my Savior and my God.

Proverbs 17:22
A cheerful heart is good medicine, but a crushed spirit dries up the bones.

Proverbs 3:5-6
Trust in the Lord with all your heart and lean not on your own understanding; in all your ways acknowledge Him, and He will make your paths straight.

DEPRESSION

<u>SCRIPTURES</u>
NEW TESTAMENT:

2 Corinthians 2:4
For I wrote you out of great distress and anguish of heart and with many tears, not to grieve you but to let you know the depth of My love for you.

Hebrews 12:3, 5
Consider him who endured such opposition from sinful men, so that you will not grow weary and lose heart. And you have forgotten that word of encouragement that addresses you as sons, My son, do not make light of the Lord's discipline, and do not lose heart when He rebukes you.

DEPRESSION

HOW TO MINISTER

THREE STEPS TO FREEDOM FROM DEPRESSION:

1. **Resist Negative Thoughts!**
   - ➢ 2 Corinthians 10:4-5

2. **Know That God Has Made You Victorious!**
   - ➢ 1 Corinthians 10:13
   - ➢ 2 Corinthians 4:8-9

3. **Change Your Thought Patterns**
   - ➢ Romans 8:35-39

<u>**Scriptures for Anxiety:**</u>
Philippians 4:6-7
1 Peter 5:7
Romans 8:28
Isaiah 26:3
John 16:33
Isaiah 49:15-16

DEPRESSION

<u>PRAYER</u>

Dear wonderful Father, I lift up _____ to You right now. You are his/her Shepherd and though he/she walks through the valley of the shadow of death, he/she will fear no evil for You are with him/her, Holy Spirit. Your Word says that Your rod and Your staff comforts them. You are the glory and the lifter of his/her head. I thank You, Lord for lifting the heaviness, the depression, the wrong focus from them right now in the mighty Name of Jesus. We declare and decree that You are their strength and hope. You are freeing them from all sorrow, from all sadness and all depression and we command it to go in Jesus' mighty Name. Lift them high above the circumstance that has brought them down and give them hope from heaven, Father. Turn their mourning into dancing and give them a song of thanksgiving for all You are doing. Bring joy now, where there was sorrow and depression. Heal every wound and every memory as You change their eyes to focus back on to You, Lord. We thank You for a miracle turnaround of supernatural joy, in Jesus' wonderful Name, Amen.

CONFUSION

<u>SCRIPTURES</u>
OLD TESTAMENT:

Psalms 71:1, 24
In You, O Lord, I have taken refuge; let me never be put to shame or confused. My tongue will tell of Your righteous acts all day long, for those who wanted to harm me have been put to shame and confusion.

Ezekiel 16:63
Then, when I make atonement for you for all you have done, you will remember and be ashamed and never again open your mouth because of your humiliation, declares the Sovereign Lord.

CONFUSION

SCRIPTURES
NEW TESTAMENT:

1 Corinthians 14:33a
For God is not a God of disorder but of peace.

2 Corinthians 10:5
We demolish arguments and every pretension that sets itself up against the knowledge of God, and we take captive every thought to make it obedient to Christ.

CONFUSION

<u>PRAYER</u>

Father, in Jesus' Name I come into agreement with
_____ for freedom from confusion. I take authority
over the disorder that is trying to bring chaos to their
mind and life. I declare a sound mind, free from
confusion, deception and torment. The realm of Your
Spirit is order and we decree order to this mind. We call
forth the mind of Christ and peace now in Jesus' mighty
Name. He/she will see and think clearly as You bring
clarity and perfect spiritual vision. You have not given
him/her a spirit of fear but of power, love and a sound
mind. I renounce confusion and command him/her to be
set free now by the blood of Jesus. Put them back on
the right path, Holy Spirit. They will be strengthened in
the power of Your might to see what You see, think what
You think, and do what You have purposed for them to
do. I thank You, Lord for healing any area of their mind
that has been under attack from the confusion. I speak
freedom now for _____, and supernatural peace.
Draw him/her near to You and let them know what Your
perfect will is for their life. They will see clearly now, in
Jesus' mighty Name, Amen.

DISCOURAGEMENT

SCRIPTURES
OLD TESTAMENT:

Deuteronomy 1:21
See, the Lord your God has given you the land. Go up and take possession of it as the Lord, the God of your fathers, told you. Do not be afraid; do not be discouraged.

2 Chronicles 32:7
Be strong and courageous. Do not be afraid or discouraged because of the king of Assyria and the vast army with him, for there is a greater power with us than with him.

Deuteronomy 31:8
The Lord himself goes before you and will be with you; He will never leave you nor forsake you. Do not be afraid; do not be discouraged.

DISCOURAGEMENT

<u>SCRIPTURES</u>
NEW TESTAMENT:

John 16:33
I have told you these things, so that in Me you may have peace. In this world you will have trouble. But take heart! I have overcome the world.

John 14:1
Do not let your hearts be troubled. Trust in God; trust also in Me.

2 Corinthians 4:16-18
Therefore we do not lose heart. Though outwardly we are wasting away, yet inwardly we are being renewed day by day. For our light and momentary troubles are achieving for us an eternal glory that far outweighs them all. So we fix our eyes not on what is seen, but on what is unseen. For what is seen is temporary, but what is unseen is eternal.

DISCOURAGEMENT

<u>PRAYER</u>

Father, I come into agreement with _____ for freedom from discouragement. You promised in Your Word to never leave him/her and have assured him/her that You will be with them until the end of the age. He/she can confidently enter Your rest and be free now from discouragement because of their faith in Your Word. Your Word covers them from being moved from that place of rest, peace and perfect trust. I decree faith to arise now, in Jesus' Name. I declare the truth and power of Your Word to overtake discouragement. I speak confidence in the Word, confidence in Your love, confidence in Your perfect will coming to pass in their life. Lord, their confidence is in You and not in the flesh. Your answers and Your promises are coming forth as he/she continues to stand on Your Word without wavering and without being moved. We know You hear him/her when they pray and we know You are moving on their behalf even now, Lord. Discouragement be broken in Jesus' Name! Confidence – come forth, peace – come forth, trust – come forth in Jesus' mighty Name. We worship You, Lord and thank You, Amen.

NEW WINE INTERNATIONAL
FEAR NOTES

DELIVERANCE

"Then you will know the truth, and the truth will set you free."

John 8:32

OPPRESSION

<u>SCRIPTURES</u>
OLD TESTAMENT:

Exodus 3:9-10
And now the cry of the Israelites has reached Me, and I have seen the way the Egyptians are oppressing them. So now, go. I am sending you to Pharaoh to bring My people the Israelites out of Egypt.

Psalm 103:6
The Lord works righteousness and justice for all the oppressed.

Psalms 146:7
He upholds the cause of the oppressed and gives food to the hungry. The Lord sets prisoners free.

OPPRESSION

SCRIPTURES
NEW TESTAMENT:

2 Corinthians 12:8-9
Three times I pleaded with the Lord to take it away from me. But He said to me, My grace is sufficient for you, for My power is made perfect in weakness. Therefore I will boast all the more gladly about my weaknesses, so that Christ's power may rest on me.

Luke 4:18-19
The Spirit of the Lord is on me, because He has anointed me to preach good news to the poor. He has sent me to proclaim freedom for the prisoners and recovery of sight for the blind, to release the oppressed, to proclaim the year of the Lord's favor.

OPPRESSION

<u>PRAYER</u>

Dear Lord, I come to You on behalf of _____. I thank You that Your Word goes out from the heavenlies and does not return to You void but accomplishes that which you please and it shall prosper in the thing for which You send it. You came to destroy the works of the enemy and delight in setting Your children free from the bondage of oppression. I ask You in the Name of Jesus and by His blood to send Your Holy Spirit to _____ and set him/her free right now from the control of this oppression. Be free! I declare freedom, that _____ be loosed and freed as You translate him/her into the Kingdom of Your dear Son, Jesus. Guide him/her into the knowledge of the truth of Your Word and help them now to see the deception and where they lost their focus on You. Remove the wrong people from their life and send people to minister Your unconditional love to them. Open their eyes and turn him/her from darkness to the light of Your love and from the deceptive power of the enemy to the matchless power of the Holy Spirit. In His wonderful Name we pray, Amen.

DEMON SPIRITS

<u>SCRIPTURES</u>
OLD TESTAMENT:

Zechariah 13:2
And it shall come to pass in that day, saith the Lord of hosts, that I will cut off the names of the idols out of the land, and they shall no more be remembered: and also I will cause the prophets and the unclean spirit to pass out of the land.

Deuteronomy 18:9-11
When thou art come into the land which the Lord thy God giveth thee, thou shalt not learn to do after the abominations of those nations. There shall not be found among you any one that maketh his son or his daughter to pass through the fire, or that useth divination, or an observer of times, or an enchanter, or a witch. Or a charmer, or a consulter with familiar spirits, or a wizard, or a necromancer.

DEMON SPIRITS

<u>SCRIPTURES</u>
NEW TESTAMENT:

Matthew 9:32-33
While they were going out, a man who was demon-possessed and could not talk was brought to Jesus. And when the demon was driven out, the man who had been mute spoke. The crowd was amazed and said, "Nothing like this has ever been seen in Israel."

Matthew 17:18
Jesus rebuked the demon, and it came out of the boy, and he was healed from that moment.

Luke 4:33,35
In the synagogue there was a man possessed by a demon, an evil spirit. He cried out at the top of his voice..."Be quiet!" Jesus said sternly. "Come out of him!" Then the demon threw the man down before them all and came out without injuring him.

DEMON SPIRITS

Here are some names used within the scriptures referring to demon spirits:

- Unclean spirit(s) – Zech. 13:2, Matt. 10:1
- Foul spirit – Mark 9:25
- Familiar spirit – Lev. 20:27, 1 Sam. 28:3
- Spirit of jealousy – Num. 5:14, Num. 5:30
- Evil spirit(s) – Luke 7:21, Acts 19:12
- Spirits – Matt. 12:45, Luke 10:20

HOW TO MINISTER

Follow these simple biblical principles when casting out demons:

1. **Bring Instruction/Teach**
   - Mark 1:21-27

2. **Tell the demon spirit(s) to "shut up"!**
   - Mark 1:15

3. **Command the demon spirit(s) to come out!**
   - Mark 1:27
   - Matthew 8:16

"And these signs will accompany those who believe: In my name they will drive out demons..."
Mark 16:17

FREEDOM FROM ADDICTIONS

"Now the Lord is the Spirit, and where the Spirit of the Lord is, there is freedom."

2 Corinthians 3:17

DRUGS

SCRIPTURES
OLD TESTAMENT:

Psalms 31:4
Free me from the trap that is set for me, for You are my refuge.

Psalms 119:45
I will walk about in freedom, for I have sought out Your precepts.

DRUGS

<u>SCRIPTURES</u>
NEW TESTAMENT:

Colossians 1:13-14
For He has rescued us from the dominion of darkness and brought us into the Kingdom of the Son He loves, in whom we have redemption, the forgiveness of sins.

Matthew 26:41
Watch and pray so that you will not fall into temptation. The spirit is willing, but the body is weak.

DRUGS

<u>PRAYER</u>

Lord Jesus, You came to set _____ free and heal the brokenhearted. If there is any sin or open door that has allowed drug addiction in his/her life, we break its power right now by the blood of Jesus and the power of agreement. If there is any unforgiveness, bitterness or offenses reveal them to him/her now so there will be repentance and complete healing. I ask You to forgive _____ for living with this bondage. I ask You to intervene in this precious life, strengthen them with Your Spirit in their inner man. I declare a healing touch from the power of God delivering them now from the bondage of these drugs. Because of Your mercy and the power of our agreement it will not have any power over him/her any longer. He/she submits their life to You completely and we thank You that the dark power of drug addiction over them is now declared totally destroyed! I thank You for peace, health and Spiritual revival in their mind, will and emotions, Lord. Remove any desire for the flesh and replace it for a desire for more of Your Presence, Lord. We need Your glory, Lord. We desire more of You, Jesus, Amen.

ALCOHOL

SCRIPTURES
OLD TESTAMENT:

Proverbs 23:19-21

Listen, My son, and be wise, and keep your heart on the right path. Do not join those who drink too much wine or gorge themselves on meat, for drunkards and gluttons become poor and drowsiness clothes them in rags.

Psalms 119:45

I will walk about in freedom, for I have sought out Your precepts.

Psalms 107:27

They reeled and staggered like drunken men; they were at their wits' end.

ALCOHOL

SCRIPTURES
NEW TESTAMENT:

Ephesians 5:15-18
Be very careful, then, how you live—not as unwise but as wise, making the most of every opportunity, because the days are evil. Therefore do not be foolish, but understand what the Lord's will is. Do not get drunk on wine, which leads to debauchery. Instead, be filled with the Spirit.

Titus 2:3
Likewise, teach the older women to be reverent in the way they live, not to be slanderers or addicted to much wine, but to teach what is good.

ALCOHOL

<u>PRAYER</u>

Dear Lord, You said You resist the proud and give grace to the humble. We come boldly before You with humble hearts, holding up _____'s need to You. We are asking for mercy and grace to help him/her in this time of need. I decree intervention for this addiction to alcohol. I declare deliverance from this bondage. We renounce alcoholism now in Jesus' mighty Name. Because of Your loving mercy it has no power over him/her any longer. You are translating him/her out from under the power of that addiction right now in by the power in the blood of Jesus. I cancel the assignment from the enemy by the mighty name of Jesus Christ. Sustain and strengthen him/her as You are completely removing this burden of addiction right now. I thank You for pouring out Your Spirit and giving him/her total victory right now, Lord. We shut the door of it ever returning and we decree this bondage broken now in Jesus' Name. Father, _____ receives Your healing touch and the deliverance You have given today. We worship and thank You, in Jesus' mighty Name, Amen.

SEXUAL

<u>SCRIPTURES</u>
OLD TESTAMENT:

Psalms 81:6
He says, I removed the burden from their shoulders; their hands were set free from the basket.

Psalms 119:9-11
How can a young man keep his way pure, by living according to Your Word. I seek You with all my heart; do not let me stray from your commands. I have hidden Your Word in my heart that I might not sin against You.

SEXUAL

SCRIPTURES
NEW TESTAMENT:

Ephesians 5: 1-3

Be imitators of God, therefore, as dearly loved children and live a life of love, just as Christ loved us and gave Himself up for us as a fragrant offering and sacrifice to God. But among you there must not be even a hint of sexual immorality, or of any kind of impurity, or of greed, because these are improper for God's holy people.

Romans 12:1-2

Therefore, I urge you, brothers, in view of God's mercy, to offer your bodies as living sacrifices, holy and pleasing to God—this is your spiritual act of worship. Do not conform any longer to the pattern of this world, but be transformed by the renewing of your mind.

SEXUAL

PRAYER

Dear Lord Jesus, we come boldly to Your throne in agreement for _____. I rebuke and renounce unhealthy sexual desires right now, in Jesus' mighty Name. I thank You for release of those thoughts, motives, and the drive to sin. I praise You for taking these desires away right now by the power of Your precious Holy Spirit. Impart Your great love and flood _____ with Your presence that satisfies every part of their being. I thank You for Your tender mercies and compassion that is renewed every morning. Forgive _____ completely for the idolatry of lust that has been put under the blood today, Lord. I ask that You put within him/her a longing for a closer walk with Your Spirit and no longer a desire to walk in the flesh. Lord, it is only through Your power and Your love that they will walk in spiritual freedom and victory so we give You praise and honor for the deliverance You have poured out today. The old nature is dead and _____ is declared alive with a new life, washed today in the precious blood of Jesus. We appropriate it by faith today and worship You as we pray in Jesus' mighty Name.

FREEDOM FROM DISOBEDIENCE

SCRIPTURES
OLD TESTAMENT:

Deuteronomy 28:1
If you fully obey the Lord your God and carefully follow all His commands I give you today, the Lord your God will set you high above all the nations on earth.

2 Chronicles 24:20
Then the Spirit of God came upon Zechariah son of Jehoiada the priest. He stood before the people and said, This is what God says: Why do you disobey the Lord's commands? You will not prosper. Because you have forsaken the Lord, He has forsaken you.

FREEDOM FROM DISOBEDIENCE

SCRIPTURES
NEW TESTAMENT:

John 8:10-11

Jesus straightened up and asked her, Woman, where are they? Has no one condemned you? No one, sir, she said. Then neither do I condemn you, Jesus declared. Go now and leave your life of sin.

Colossians 1:21-22

Once you were alienated from God and were enemies in your minds because of your evil behavior. But now He has reconciled you by Christ's physical body through death to present you holy in His sight, without blemish and free from accusation.

FREEDOM FROM DISOBEDIENCE

<u>PRAYER</u>

Dear heavenly Father, thank You for forgiving _____ completely today as we come before You for forgiveness for his/her willful disobedience. Teach us all to obey Your commandments quickly, without questioning, Lord. Change his/her reactions that have been to disobey and work in him/her new responses of total trust and obedience. Lord, You have commanded him/her to turn from iniquity and rebellion and have promised that he/she will spend his/her days in prosperity as they obey Your Word. Your Word is life and truth and a light unto his/her path. I decree a new heart for _____ and a new desire to walk by Your Spirit and not by their flesh or emotions. Speak to them, Lord and they will delight to follow Your voice like never before! I declare new freedom, a new revelation of how rebellion has led them in the past. Touch him/her right now and begin the mighty new work through their repentant heart and willingness to change. Thank You for this miracle, Lord Jesus, Amen.

FREEDOM FROM ANGER/BITTERNESS

<u>SCRIPTURES</u>
OLD TESTAMENT:

Psalms 37:8-9
Refrain from anger and turn from wrath; do not fret—it leads only to evil. For evil men will be cut off, but those who hope in the Lord will inherit the land.

Proverbs 14:29
A patient man has great understanding, but a quick-tempered man displays folly.

Ezekiel 36:26
I will give you a new heart and put a new spirit in you; I will remove from you your heart of stone and give you a heart of flesh.

127

FREEDOM FROM ANGER/BITTERNESS

SCRIPTURES
NEW TESTAMENT:

Hebrews 12:15
See to it that no one misses the grace of God and that no bitter root grows up to cause trouble and defile many.

Ephesians 4:26-27, 31-32
In your anger do not sin. Do not let the sun go down while you are still angry, and do not give the devil a foothold. Get rid of all bitterness, rage and anger, brawling and slander, along with every form of malice. Be kind and compassionate to one another, forgiving each other, just as in Christ God forgave you.

James 5:16
Therefore confess your sins to each other and pray for each other so that you may be healed. The prayer of a righteous man is powerful and effective.

FREEDOM FROM ANGER/BITTERNESS

<u>PRAYER</u>

Dear Lord, I stand in agreement for _____ who confesses and desires to be set free from anger and bitterness. I ask You to forgive him/her for holding bitterness against others. I ask You to work forgiveness in their own heart they may be holding toward their own self. I ask You to work in their heart real forgiveness because _____ has held anger and bitterness toward others. I pray for a brand new heart and a new spirit to be placed within him/her right now, setting him/her free from anger and unforgiveness. This is a new day that You have prepared for him/her, Lord and we receive Your miracle touch for _____ right now in Jesus' Name. Let Your glory shine down on them, giving them hope, healing and a heart of flesh that only You can give. He/she will be slow to anger and have a soft answer now that will turn away wrath even in his/her own life. Help him/her to minister to those You bring across their path that need a healing in this area. Let this precious life be a witness of Your miracle working power, Lord, in Jesus' Name, Amen.

FREEDOM FROM TEMPTATION

SCRIPTURES
OLD TESTAMENT:

Proverbs 1:10
My son, if sinners entice you, do not give in to them.

Proverbs 4:11-15
I guide you in the way of wisdom and lead you along straight paths. When you walk, your steps will not be hampered; when you run, you will not stumble. Hold on to instruction; do not let it go. Guard it well, for it is your life. Do not set foot on the path of the wicked or walk in the way of evil men. Avoid it, do not travel on it; turn from it and go on your way.

FREEDOM FROM TEMPTATION

SCRIPTURES
NEW TESTAMENT:

Luke 11:3-5
Give us each day our daily bread. Forgive us our sins, for we also forgive everyone who sins against us. And lead us not into temptation but deliver us from evil.

1 Corinthians 10:14
Therefore, my dear friends, flee from idolatry.

Matthew 6:13
And lead us not into temptation, but deliver us from the evil one.

FREEDOM FROM TEMPTATION

<u>PRAYER</u>

Father, I pray right now for _____ who has come to You for help. You said we are not given more than we can bear so he/she is asking for strength and Your overcoming power right now. You are faithful to answer those who call upon You and right now we declare that Your strength is sufficient in their weakness. Remove their weakness right now, Lord and replace it with supernatural strength to do Your will. He/she will know where to walk and where not to walk; You are opening their eyes by removing the blinders. Let them recognize the wrong path and see the right path You have laid before them. I ask for Your Spirit to be poured without measure on _____ right now and that they will run quickly from temptation and not give in any longer. I thank You Father for the miracle You are working in their life right now, that You have already won this battle and they can worship and thank You right now. You are his/her defense, their rock and fortress and we thank You for it Lord, in Jesus' Name, Amen.

FREEDOM FROM COMPLAINING

SCRIPTURES
OLD TESTAMENT:

Numbers 11:1

Now the people complained about their hardships in the hearing of the Lord, and when He heard them His anger was aroused. Then fire from the Lord burned among them and consumed some of the outskirts of the camp.

Exodus 16:8

Moses also said, You will know that it was the Lord when He gives you meat to eat in the evening and all the bread you want in the morning, because He has heard your grumbling against Him. Who are we? You are not grumbling against us, but against the Lord.

FREEDOM FROM COMPLAINING

<u>SCRIPTURES</u>
NEW TESTAMENT:

Philippians 2:14-16
Do everything without complaining or arguing, so that you may become blameless and pure, children of God without fault in a crooked and depraved generation, in which you shine like stars in the universe as you hold out the word of life—in order that I may boast on the day of Christ that I did not run or labor for nothing.

Jude 16
These men are grumblers and faultfinders; they follow their own evil desires; they boast about themselves and flatter others for their own advantage.

FREEDOM FROM COMPLAINING

PRAYER

Dear heavenly Father, _____ and I are coming to You in time of need. Lord, he/she has recognized the need for intervention. As he/she repents of this habit that has displeased You, Lord, so we ask for Your help and Your healing touch. Your precious Spirit is ministering to him/her right now with a change of mind, a change of heart. Put a spirit of thanksgiving in their heart, a new joy and a new walk of faith. He/she desires to please You, Father, so remove the old habits and replace them with a new outlook, new responses. As he/she turns to look at You, let there be renewed strength and an even greater supernatural faith to come upon him/her. I thank You for a new attitude of praise and thanksgiving that begins even now to spring up. Where there was depression and complaining, I thank You for new faith, new vision and new joy. Restore the years the enemy has stolen and revive this precious heart. We thank You for all You're doing, in Jesus' Name, Amen.

FREEDOM FROM GUILT

SCRIPTURES
OLD TESTAMENT:

Psalms 32:1
Blessed is he whose transgressions are forgiven, whose sins are covered.

Psalms 51:1-2
Have mercy on me, O God, according to Your unfailing love; according to Your great compassion blot out my transgressions. Wash away all my iniquity and cleanse me from my sin.

FREEDOM FROM GUILT

<u>SCRIPTURES</u>
NEW TESTAMENT:

Romans 8:1
Therefore, there is now no condemnation for those who are in Christ Jesus.

Romans 8:33
Who will bring any charge against those whom God has chosen? It is God who justifies.

Romans 3:24
We are justified freely by His grace through the redemption that came by Christ Jesus.

FREEDOM FROM GUILT

PRAYER

Dear precious Jesus, You said if we confess our sins, You are faithful to forgive us from those sins. _____ has confessed he/she has carried guilt and desires to be freed right now. Thank You for forgiving him/her of him/her iniquities and for remembering them no more. You have removed the sins from him/her as far as the east is from the west. Help him/her to be like You and not remember them as You have buried them under the blood of Your dear Son, Jesus. From this day forward I declare _____ is free from guilt and it has no dominion over his/her life. You have set him/her free this day and cleansed him/her from all sin and now it is as if he/she had never sinned. Thank You, Lord for a new life, a new outlook, a new vision and that vision is of You, Lord. Thank You for a new day of freedom and renewed joy. Thank You that he/she can worship You without looking back but by looking unto Jesus the author and finisher of his/her faith. You are worthy to be praised and we worship You in the Name of Jesus, Amen.

FREEDOM FROM THE OCCULT

<u>SCRIPTURES</u>
OLD TESTAMENT:

Psalms 142:7

Set me free from my prison, that I may praise Your Name. Then the righteous will gather about me because of Your goodness to me.

Ezekiel 13:20

Therefore this is what the Sovereign Lord says: I am against your magic charms with which you ensnare people like birds and I will tear them from your arms; I will set free the people that you ensnare like birds.

FREEDOM FROM THE OCCULT

SCRIPTURES
NEW TESTAMENT:

Ephesians 6:10-12

Finally, be strong in the Lord and in His mighty power. Put on the full armor of God so that you can take your stand against the devil's schemes. For our struggle is not against flesh and blood, but against the rulers, against the authorities, against the powers of this dark world and against the spiritual forces of evil in the heavenly realms.

1 Peter 2:9

But you are a chosen people, a royal priesthood, a holy nation, a people belonging to God, that you may declare the praises of Him who called you out of darkness into His wonderful light.

FREEDOM FROM THE OCCULT

PRAYER

Dear Lord Jesus, You came to destroy the works of darkness and _____ confesses right now he/she has been a part of spiritual darkness. Shine the light of Your Spirit on this dark area of his/her life right now, Lord and we rebuke and destroy the principalities and powers that have been at work in their life. I ask You by the Name above all Names, Jesus Christ, and by His blood that you set _____ free right now and loosed from all occultism and spiritual wickedness. Impart a fresh infilling and overflowing of the Holy Spirit. I declare he/she is free now and delivered from the power of darkness and is translated into the glorious Kingdom of Your Son, Jesus Christ. We know You delight in setting the captives free and taking back the spoils of the enemy. Right now we worship You for the power that is in the blood and the authority You have given _____ through Jesus' obedience on the cross. He/she will be strong in the Lord and in His mighty power and worship You for what You have done for him/her today! In Jesus' precious Name we pray, Amen.

FREEDOM FROM SUICIDE

FACTS

In 2006, suicide was the eleventh leading cause of death in the U.S., claiming 33,300 lives per year. Suicide rates among youth (15-24) have increased more than 200% in the last fifty years. The suicide rate is also very high for the elderly, accounting for almost 16% of all suicides.[3]

It is estimated that there are more than 1,000 suicides on college campuses per year.

Every 2 hours and 5 minutes, a person under the age of 25 completes suicide.

Suicide rates for children between the ages of 10-14 increased over 50% between 1981 and 2006.

Suicide is preventable. Most suicidal people desperately want to live; they are just unable to see alternatives to their problems. Most suicidal people give definite warning signals of their deadly intentions.

---

[3] All statistics received from American Association of Suicidology.
www.NewWineInternational.org

FREEDOM FROM SUICIDE

<u>SCRIPTURES</u>
OLD TESTAMENT:

Deuteronomy 30:19-20

This day I call heaven and earth as witnesses against you that I have set before you life and death, blessings and curses. Now choose life, so that you and your children may live and that you may love the Lord your God, listen to His voice, and hold fast to Him. For the Lord is your life, and He will give you many years in the land He swore to give to your fathers, Abraham, Isaac and Jacob.

Proverbs 1:32

For the waywardness of the simple will kill them, and the complacency of fools will destroy them.

FREEDOM FROM SUICIDE

SCRIPTURES
NEW TESTAMENT:

Galatians 3:13
Christ redeemed us from the curse of the law by becoming a curse for us, for it is written: Cursed is everyone who is hung on a tree.

2 Corinthians 3:16-17
But whenever anyone turns to the Lord, the veil is taken away. Now the Lord is the Spirit, and where the Spirit of the Lord is, there is freedom.

John 10:18
No one takes My life from me, but I lay it down of My own accord. I have authority to lay it down and authority to take it up again. This command I received from My Father.

FREEDOM FROM SUICIDE

<u>PRAYER</u>

Dear heavenly Father, _____ and I come to You with boldness. We renounce all suicidal thoughts and any attempts he/she has made to take his/her own life or in any way injure him/her own self. I renounce the lie that he/she believed that life is hopeless. You came to give him/her life and life more abundantly. Thank You that he/she has chosen life by repenting and asking for prayer, so right now in the Name of Jesus Christ of Nazareth, we appropriate that life to _____. We cancel the assignment from hell, the assignment of death by the power of the blood of Jesus. You are the glory and the lifter of his/her head, placing a wall of fire round about him/her. Assign a guardian angel that encamps around all those who fear You and You shall deliver them. I decree deliverance and declare new life for _____, with a new joy for the future! You are his/her fortress now, Lord, translating him/her out of the realm of darkness into Your ream of freedom in Jesus. We worship You and thank You for what You have done today, in Jesus' Name, Amen.

BREAKING GENERATIONAL CURSES

<u>SCRIPTURES</u>
OLD TESTAMENT:

Leviticus 26:40-41
But if they will confess their sins and the sins of their fathers—their treachery against Me and their hostility toward Me, which made Me hostile toward them so that I sent them into the land of their enemies—then when their uncircumcised hearts are humbled and they pay for their sin.

Deuteronomy 30:19-20
This day I call heaven and earth as witnesses against you that I have set before you life and death, blessings and curses. Now choose life, so that you and your children may live and that you may love the Lord your God, listen to His voice, and hold fast to Him. For the Lord is your life, and He will give you many years in the land He swore to give to your fathers, Abraham, Isaac and Jacob.

BREAKING GENERATIONAL CURSES

SCRIPTURES
NEW TESTAMENT:

Galatians 3:13
Christ redeemed us from the curse of the law by becoming a curse for us, for it is written: Cursed is everyone who is hung on a tree.

2 Corinthians 3:16-17
But whenever anyone turns to the Lord, the veil is taken away. Now the Lord is the Spirit, and where the Spirit of the Lord is, there is freedom.

BREAKING GENERATIONAL CURSES

<u>PRAYER</u>

Lord Jesus, I lift up _____ to You in the matchless Name of Jesus. By authority of the Blood of the Lamb we rebuke and cancel any and all curses that have been present over this life and this family. We thank You Jesus that You redeemed us from the curse and became a curse for us on the cross. No longer will a generational curse have dominion over _____. He/she has taken the dominion back and chosen life by repenting for walking in darkness. He/she and his/her children, family and descendants will now live and love the Lord their God, hearing only His voice, and holding fast to Him. I thank You for newness of life, the old has been done away with and he/she has been washed clean by the Blood of the Lamb today. I thank You for the mind of Christ, new visions, new dreams, for a future that is as bright as Your glory, Lord. I declare them free by the power of God's Holy Spirit. For where the Spirit of the Lord is there is liberty. In Jesus' wonderful Name we pray, Amen.

RENEWING THE MIND

<u>SCRIPTURES</u>
OLD TESTAMENT:

Jeremiah 7:5-7
If you really change your ways and your actions and deal with each other justly, if you do not oppress the alien, the fatherless or the widow and do not shed innocent blood in this place, and if you do not follow other gods to your own harm, then I will let you live in this place, in the land I gave your forefathers forever and ever.

1 Chronicles 28:9
And you, My son Solomon, acknowledge the God of your father, and serve Him with wholehearted devotion and with a willing mind, for the Lord searches every heart and understands every motive behind the thoughts. If you seek Him, He will be found by you; but if you forsake Him, He will reject you forever.

RENEWING THE MIND

<u>SCRIPTURES</u>
NEW TESTAMENT:

Ephesians 4:22-24
You were taught, with regard to your former way of life, to put off your old self, which is being corrupted by its deceitful desires; to be made new in the attitude of your minds; and to put on the new self, created to be like God in true righteousness and holiness.

Romans 12:2
Do not conform any longer to the pattern of this world, but be transformed by the renewing of your mind. Then you will be able to test and approve what God's will is—His good, pleasing and perfect will.

RENEWING THE MIND

<u>PRAYER</u>

Dear Lord Jesus, thank You for the renewing process that is taking place right now in the mind of _____. He/she looks not to the things that are seen but to the things that are unseen, those things from the heavenly realm of Your Word, the things that are unseen but are eternal. I pray in agreement for him/her to be continually renewed in their mind by the washing of the water of Your Word. I pray that their mind is being transformed right now to see with Your eyes, Lord. I declare a turnaround, a breakthrough for _____ that gives them renewed hope and a future that lines up with Your perfect will, Father. Thank You it is done, right now in Jesus' mighty Name. He/she will set her mind on Your Word and obey Your Word, thinking Your thoughts, believing Your Words and trusting in Your voice. Cause his/her reactions to change and new responses to spring up out of his/her spirit. Lord, remind him/her that Your voice is all that matters and the voices of others he/she can silence by walking in Your glorious truth in love. Thank You for a powerful testimony, Lord. We worship You and thank You, in Jesus' mighty Name, Amen.

WALKING IN VICTORY

<u>SCRIPTURES</u>
OLD TESTAMENT:

Isaiah 25:8

He will swallow up death forever. The Sovereign Lord will wipe away the tears from all faces; He will remove the disgrace of His people from all the earth. The Lord has spoken.

Psalms 98:1

Sing to the Lord a new song, for He has done marvelous things; His right hand and His holy arm have worked salvation for Him.

WALKING IN VICTORY

SCRIPTURES
NEW TESTAMENT:

Philippians 4:9
Whatever you have learned or received or heard from Me, or seen in Me—put it into practice. And the God of peace will be with you.

1 Corinthians 15:55-57
Where, O death, is your victory? Where, O death, is your sting? The sting of death is sin, and the power of sin is the law. But thanks be to God! He gives us the victory through our Lord Jesus Christ.

WALKING IN VICTORY

<u>PRAYER</u>

Dear Father, we thank You for You are the victory in every area of our lives. I stand in agreement right now with _____ who desires to walk in Your victory. I speak victory right now into his/her life by the power of Jesus; he/she is free from weakness, insecurity and defeat. There is no room for doubt in his/her life when the spirit of faith is present so we ask You, Holy Spirit to give him/her a fresh, new infilling of Your Spirit. Overflow them with supernatural faith and strength, Father. Because of the victory You purchased on the cross for _____, he/she will be steadfast and immovable, abounding in Your truth and power. Because of the victory You are giving them today, Lord, they will live secure knowing that nothing shall be able to separate them from Your great infinite love. I cancel all defeat and doubt once and for all in _____'s life and declare freedom and newness of life. I decree new strength to be evident in this life today, Lord. We thank You in the mighty Name of Jesus, Amen.

DESTINY

"For I know the plans I have for you," declares the Lord, "plans to prosper you and not to harm you, plans to give you hope and a future."

Jeremiah 29:11

WHEN ALL LOOKS HOPELESS

<u>SCRIPTURES</u>
OLD TESTAMENT:

Psalms 25:5
Guide me in Your truth and teach me, for You are God my Savior, and my hope is in You all day long.

Zechariah 9:12
Return to your fortress, O prisoners of hope; even now I announce that I will restore twice as much to you.

WHEN ALL LOOKS HOPELESS

SCRIPTURES
NEW TESTAMENT:

Romans 15:13

May the God of hope fill you with all joy and peace as you trust in Him, so that you may overflow with hope by the power of the Holy Spirit.

Romans 4:18

Against all hope, Abraham in hope believed and so became the father of many nations, just as it had been said to him, so shall your offspring be.

Colossians 1:27

To them God has chosen to make known among the Gentiles the glorious riches of this mystery, which is Christ in you, the hope of glory.

WHEN ALL LOOKS HOPELESS

PRAYER

Dear Lord, I lift up _____ to You and pray right now for an impartation of renewed hope to spring forth in their life. You are the God of hope and You said You would fill us with all joy and peace as we trust in You, so that we may overflow with hope by Holy Spirit's glorious power. Thank You for new visions and new dreams of a future that is attainable through Your Son, Jesus Christ. The hope You imparted today will prevent him/her from being moved out of that place of trusting in Your Word. When You say it, You mean it and we believe You and trust You totally. Your Word declares that Christ in _____ is the hope of glory. Continue to fill them with Your hope enabling them to glorify You despite their circumstances. In the future when all looks hopeless, they will remember Your Word and remember to walk in faith and remember that You are their hope. Fill them with joy now and the promise that You will never leave them or forsake them. We believe Your Word, Lord and rejoice that Your Word is forever settled in heaven, in the powerful Name of Jesus, Amen.

www.NewWineInternational.org

THE WILL OF GOD

<u>SCRIPTURES</u>
OLD TESTAMENT:

Psalms 40:8
I desire to do Your will, O my God; Your law is within my heart.

Proverbs 16:9
In his heart a man plans his course, but the Lord determines his steps.

Proverbs 19:20-21
Listen to advice and accept instruction, and in the end you will be wise. Many are the plans in a man's heart, but it is the Lord's purpose that prevails.

THE WILL OF GOD

SCRIPTURES
NEW TESTAMENT:

Romans 8:28
And we know that in all things God works for the good of those who love Him, who have been called according to His purpose.

Luke 22:42
Father, if You are willing, take this cup from Me; yet not my will, but Yours be done.

Matthew 12:50
For whoever does the will of My Father in heaven is My brother and sister and mother.

THE WILL OF GOD

PRAYER

Father, in the Name of Jesus, we come to You and lift up _____. He/she delights to know Your will and to do Your will. Thank You that You have a plan and a purpose for him/her that is for good and not for evil, for prosperity and peace and power. Forgive him/her for the times they have led their own life and left the security of Your perfect will and plan. He/she repents of all the self-will in their life so cause them now to remember that they can do nothing apart from You, Father. Reveal the direction and the purpose You have for _____. Holy Spirit, speak to him/her and confirm Your Word with signs following. Their life is to be a sign and a wonder so Father speak for Your servant is listening. Silence the voices around them and quicken the words You have spoken in the past. Resurrect old visions and dreams, Lord, and resurrect the plan that even laid dormant waiting for this moment. I decree purpose to spring forth, declare the will of God to be revealed in Jesus' mighty Name. You will make the mysteries of Your will known unto them, according to Your good pleasure. Thank You, Lord Jesus, Amen.

DESTINY DOORS

<u>SCRIPTURES</u>
OLD TESTAMENT:

Psalm 24:7-10

Lift up your heads, O you gates; be lifted up, you ancient doors, that the King of glory may come in. Who is this King of glory? The Lord strong and mighty, the Lord mighty in battle. Lift up your heads, O you gates; lift them up, you ancient doors, that the King of glory may come in. Who is He, this King of glory? The Lord Almighty— He is the King of glory.

Isaiah 22:22

I will place on his shoulder the key to the house of David; what he opens no one can shut, and what he shuts no one can open.

DESTINY DOORS

<u>SCRIPTURES</u>
NEW TESTAMENT:

Matthew 7:7-8
"Ask and it will be given to you; seek and you will find; knock and the door will be opened to you. For everyone who asks receives; he who seeks finds; and to him who knocks, the door will be opened."

Luke 11:9-10
"So I say to you: Ask and it will be given to you; seek and you will find; knock and the door will be opened to you. For everyone who asks receives; he who seeks finds; and to him who knocks, the door will be opened."

Revelation 3:8
I know your deeds. See, I have placed before you an open door that no one can shut. I know that you have little strength, yet you have kept my word and have not denied my name.

FRUITFULNESS

"This is to my Father's glory, that you bear much fruit, showing yourselves to be my disciples."

John 15:8

WALKING IN LOVE

<u>SCRIPTURES</u>
OLD TESTAMENT:

Psalms 119:41, 76
May your unfailing love come to me, O Lord, Your salvation according to Your promise; May Your unfailing love be my comfort, according to Your promise to Your servant.

Deuteronomy 10:12
And now, O Israel, what does the Lord your God ask of you but to fear the Lord your God, to walk in all His ways, to love Him, to serve the Lord your God with all your heart and with all your soul.

WALKING IN LOVE

<u>SCRIPTURES</u>
NEW TESTAMENT:

Romans 8:37
No, in all these things we are more than conquerors through Him who loved us.

1 John 4:18-19
There is no fear in love. But perfect love drives out fear, because fear has to do with punishment. The one who fears is not made perfect in love. We love because He first loved us.

1 John 4:16
And so we know and rely on the love God has for us. God is love. Whoever lives in love lives in God, and God in him.

WALKING IN LOVE

PRAYER

Dear Lord Jesus, You are love and there is no fear in love because perfect love cast out all fear. We love You, Lord because You first loved us. I ask You right now to cover _____ with a warm blanket of Your love, Jesus. Forgive us for the times we acted in fear, the times we were unlovely to others and show us how to walk in unconditional love as You do. Show us how to walk in love when everyone around us is being unkind and unlovely. We want to experience Your love right now, Jesus, so supernaturally release that love right now on _____. There is no limit to Your love, Lord, so pour out Your love on him/her in unlimited measures. Right now I decree he/she receives an overflowing dose of that love, going down into the depths of his/her being. Love is the most excellent way and You want us to walk in that love at all times. Teach us to love others as well as ourselves as You love, Lord. Your love gives us purpose for giving and purpose for living, and always leads us to greater joy. Thank You for imparting Your love right now, in Jesus' Name, Amen.

WALKING IN JOY

<u>SCRIPTURES</u>
OLD TESTAMENT:

Proverbs 15:15
All the days of the oppressed are wretched, but the cheerful heart has a continual feast.

Deuteronomy 28:47-48
Because you did not serve the Lord your God joyfully and gladly in the time of prosperity, therefore in hunger and thirst, in nakedness and dire poverty, you will serve the enemies the Lord sends against you.

Psalms 118:24
This is the day the Lord has made; let us rejoice and be glad in it.

WALKING IN JOY

SCRIPTURES
NEW TESTAMENT:

Romans 14:17
For the Kingdom of God is not a matter of eating and drinking, but of righteousness, peace and joy in the Holy Spirit.

Hebrews 12:2
Let us fix our eyes on Jesus, the author and perfecter of our faith, who for the joy set before Him endured the cross, scorning its shame, and sat down at the right hand of the throne of God.

James 1:2
Consider it pure joy, my brothers, whenever you face trials of many kinds.

WALKING IN JOY

PRAYER

I lift up _____ to You right now as he/she faces this situation that is trying to steal his/her joy. Your joy is our strength, so I ask You to give him/her a double dose of Your glorious joy right now that they will be strong in this hour of testing. You have given us joy unspeakable and full of glory Lord, so we count it all joy when we are faced with trials. I decree _____ be full of that special joy that comes from trusting in You, Lord, that You hold everything in the palm of Your hand. This is the day You have made and we choose to rejoice and be exceedingly glad in it. We choose to let go of the fears and concerns that steal our joy and we declare that weight lifting now off _____. A merry heart does good like medicine and we receive that medicine of Your love for him/her right now and release Your immeasurable joy. May it overflow out of him/her onto others as they witness the salvation of the Lord. They will praise You all the days of their life and worship in the beauty of Your holiness, love and joy. Amen.

WALKING IN PEACE

<u>SCRIPTURES</u>
OLD TESTAMENT:

Isaiah 26:3
You will keep in perfect peace him whose mind is steadfast, because he trusts in You.

Isaiah 57:2
Those who walk uprightly enter into peace; they find rest as they lie in death.

WALKING IN PEACE

<u>SCRIPTURES</u>
NEW TESTAMENT:

John 14:27

Peace I leave with you; my peace I give you. I do not give to you as the world gives. Do not let your hearts be troubled and do not be afraid.

Colossians 3:15

Let the peace of Christ rule in your hearts, since as members of one body you were called to peace. And be thankful.

Philippians 4:7

And the peace of God, which transcends all understanding, will guard your hearts and your minds in Christ Jesus.

WALKING IN PEACE

<u>PRAYER</u>

Dear Father, I lift up _____ to You right now in agreement for peace in his/her life. Where there is turmoil, Lord, bring peace. Where there is confusion, Lord, bring Your peace. Where there is fear, Lord, bring even more peace. I ask You to blanket them right now with Your presence which is their peace and comfort. I speak quiet to their mind, quiet to their heart, quiet to the voices around them and bring them a supernatural measure of Your Divine peace. You will keep him/her in perfect peace as their mind is fixed on You, Father. Help him/her to know and follow that peace which passes all understanding. Keep their tongue from causing others to fear by speaking words that You have not spoken. Help him/her to be mindful of the peace they can impart to others, even as they receive peace from You, Lord. Let Your supernatural peace flow like a river now, flooding their very being with Your peace. Thank You, Jesus, for leaving Your peace for _____ through the precious Holy Spirit. In Jesus' Name we pray, Amen.

WALKING IN PATIENCE

<u>SCRIPTURES</u>
OLD TESTAMENT:

Psalms 40:1-3

I waited patiently for the Lord; He turned to me and heard my cry. He lifted me out of the slimy pit, out of the mud and mire; He set my feet on a rock and gave me a firm place to stand. He put a new song in my mouth, a hymn of praise to our God. Many will see and fear and put their trust in the Lord.

Ecclesiastes 7:8-9

The end of a matter is better than its beginning, and patience is better than pride. Do not be quickly provoked in your spirit, for anger resides in the lap of fools.

WALKING IN PATIENCE

SCRIPTURES
NEW TESTAMENT:

Romans 8:25
But if we hope for what we do not yet have, we wait for it patiently.

Hebrews 10:36
You need to persevere so that when you have done the will of God, you will receive what He has promised.

Hebrews 6:12
We do not want you to become lazy, but to imitate those who through faith and patience inherit what has been promised.

WALKING IN PATIENCE

<u>PRAYER</u>

Dear precious Lord, I ask in the Name of Jesus for patience for _____. As You are covering any anxious thoughts with peace, let the glory of God flow to him/her right now. Your timing is perfect; we know that and trust You in the plans and purposes You have for this precious man/lady. Help him/her to remember that the end of a matter is better than the beginning and that a patient spirit is better than a proud spirit. Help him/her to run their race with patient endurance, the race You have set before them, looking unto You for the perfect timing and perfect plan. Your peace is flowing to them right now, causing them to let go of trying to figure out how, when, who, what and where. You are sufficient, You are all in all and You are more than enough. Focusing on You and breathing in Your presence will continue to dispel the anxiety or worry that accompanies impatience. Impart and teach patience to _____ as You work out all the details of their life. Trusting You with our whole heart is our honor and we do it with grace and faith, in Jesus' Name, Amen.

WALKING IN GENTLENESS

SCRIPTURES
OLD TESTAMENT:

Proverbs 15:1
A gentle answer turns away wrath, but a harsh word stirs up anger.

Ecclesiastes 10:4
If a ruler's anger rises against you, do not leave your post; calmness can lay great errors to rest.

WALKING IN GENTLENESS

SCRIPTURES
NEW TESTAMENT:

Peter 3:4
Instead, it should be that of your inner self, the unfading beauty of a gentle and quiet spirit, which is of great worth in God's sight.

Titus 3:2
To slander no one, to be peaceable and considerate, and to show true humility toward all men.

Ephesians 4:2
Be completely humble and gentle; be patient, bearing with one another in love.

WALKING IN GENTLENESS

PRAYER

Father God, You are gentle and gracious and I come into agreement for _____ to receive from You a piece of Your nature today. Forgive him/her for the times they have grown agitated, anxious and impatient. Impart a meek and quiet spirit to them by Your power and authority in their life that will strengthen them for their life's challenges. They submit their life to You today and ask for a miracle, a breakthrough, a change of heart. Sweeten their relationships and dealings with others, especially those who are not as lovely as You, Lord. Sprinkle a big dose of Your gentle love on them, that covers the agitation of life. Deliver them from rudeness in relationships and acquaintances, especially with those who disappoint them. We trust You with our lives, Lord and trust that You are supernaturally touching _____ this day. Thank You for Your gentle spirit, Your kindness, Your meekness and Your strength. We believe You are doing miracles for _____ and praise Your Name for the victory, in Jesus' Name, Amen.

WALKING IN GOODNESS

<u>SCRIPTURES</u>
OLD TESTAMENT:

Psalms 23:6
Surely goodness and love will follow me all the days of my life, and I will dwell in the house of the Lord forever.

Psalms 145:7
They will celebrate Your abundant goodness and joyfully sing of Your righteousness.

WALKING IN GOODNESS

SCRIPTURES
NEW TESTAMENT:

Romans 7:18

I know that nothing good lives in me, that is, in my sinful nature. For I have the desire to do what is good, but I cannot carry it out.

Romans 15:14

I myself am convinced, my brothers, that you yourselves are full of goodness, complete in knowledge and competent to instruct one another.

2 Peter 1:5

For this very reason, make every effort to add to your faith goodness; and to goodness, knowledge.

WALKING IN GOODNESS

PRAYER

Heavenly Father, all goodness comes from You so I lift up _____ to You today and ask for an impartation of Your goodness. How great is Your goodness that has been laid up in store for those who fear You. _____ fears You today and rejoices in the mighty testimonies they have been given by Your goodness and Your mercy. Lord, satisfy the longing of his/her soul for Your goodness today as he/she walks in Your ways. May Your goodness lead them into a closer walk and deeper knowledge of You. As they endeavor to walk in the light of Your Word, You are filling them even now with Your goodness, righteousness and truth. I rejoice that Your life in him/her produces the fruit of goodness in their live. Continue to cause them to hunger after You, Your Word and Your ways. May Your goodness follow them all the days of their life. We praise You for it, Lord, in the mighty Name of Jesus, Amen.

WALKING IN FAITHFULNESS

SCRIPTURES
OLD TESTAMENT:

Lamentations 3:23
Because of the Lord's great love we are not consumed, for His compassions never fail. They are new every morning; great is Your faithfulness.

Proverbs 28:20
A faithful man will be richly blessed, but one eager to get rich will not go unpunished.

WALKING IN FAITHFULNESS

SCRIPTURES
NEW TESTAMENT:

Galatians 5:22

But the fruit of the Spirit is love, joy, peace, patience, kindness, goodness, faithfulness.

Matthew 25:23

His master replied, Well done, good and faithful servant! You have been faithful with a few things; I will put you in charge of many things. Come and share your master's happiness!

WALKING IN FAITHFULNESS

<u>PRAYER</u>

Dear precious Lord, I ask that You reveal Your awesome faithfulness to _____ in the Name of Jesus. As he/she is reminded of Your unending faithfulness to him/her in the past, impart that same walk of faithfulness to him/her. They are asking You for steadiness, consistency, stability to be worked into his/her life. Teach them Your priorities, the power of their spoken word, the unending Covenant You have with them. Teach them that when they give their word, it is written on Your heart. Thank You for Your faithful mercies that are new every morning. Your loving kindness to him/her is renewed each day. Show _____ what is necessary to do each day to continue to cause this fruit of the Spirit to develop fully in this life. As You have touched them this day, may it be just the beginning of a powerful turnaround for them and for those close to them. We thank You, Lord and praise Your Name forever because of Your faithfulness. In Jesus' mighty Name, Amen.

WALKING IN MEEKNESS

<u>SCRIPTURES</u>
OLD TESTAMENT:

Numbers 12:3

Now Moses was a very humble man, more humble than anyone else on the face of the earth.

Proverbs 15:33

The fear of the Lord teaches a man wisdom, and humility comes before honor.

WALKING IN MEEKNESS

SCRIPTURES
NEW TESTAMENT:

Matthew 11:29

Take My yoke upon you and learn from Me, for I am gentle and humble in heart, and you will find rest for your souls.

Ephesians 4:1

As a prisoner for the Lord, then, I urge you to live a life worthy of the calling you have received.

WALKING IN MEEKNESS

<u>PRAYER</u>

Father, I lift up _____ to You right now in Jesus' Name. As Your servant and son, I ask You to begin the work now of teaching him/her how to walk in meekness, the quality of the fruit of the Spirit that is pliable, teachable and submissive to Your Word and full of grace. Lord, _____ desires to put on the new man today and with Your supernatural power I ask You to begin now, Father. Help them to be slow to take offense at others and to patiently endure even when he/she is wrongfully persecuted. We expect this gentle meekness to begin to grow in them daily. They choose to walk worthy of the calling to which they have been called by You to bring You glory and honor. We expect change, we expect a complete work, we expect humility to spring forth even now as they lay their burdens at Your feet and trust You completely, for You are the answer and the door. We thank You ahead of time for this great work that has begun and worship You for You are meek and lowly and full of wisdom and strength. In the mighty Name of Jesus we pray, Amen.

WALKING IN SELF-CONTROL

SCRIPTURES
OLD TESTAMENT:

Proverbs 25:28
Like a city whose walls are broken down is a man who lacks self-control.

Proverbs 16:32
Better a patient man than a warrior, a man who controls his temper than one who takes a city.

WALKING IN SELF-CONTROL

SCRIPTURES
NEW TESTAMENT:

Galatians 5:22-23
But the fruit of the Spirit is love, joy, peace, patience, kindness, goodness, faithfulness, gentleness and self-control. Against such things there is no law.

2 Timothy 1:7
For God did not give us a spirit of timidity, but a spirit of power, of love and of self-discipline.

WALKING IN SELF-CONTROL

PRAYER

Dear Father, I lift up to You _____ who recognizes the great need for self control in his/her life. He/she needs supernatural help from You, Lord, as they need patience and temperance to finish the race You have set before them. Strengthen them now, Lord, by Your precious Holy Spirit and begin that mighty work in their life. We thank You, Father, and ask You to infuse temperance, self control and knowledge into their walk right now. Show him/her any areas that remain out of control and show him/her any open doors or areas that may need to be repented for, known or unknown. Help _____ to walk in temperance and give him/her a renewed love for Your Word. Cover him/her with Your blood today, Father, and wash them clean and white as snow. Remove all traces of guilt or condemnation as they walk forth now in newness of life. We trust You for the work that has begun and pray in the matchless Name of Jesus, Amen.

SALVATION

"For it is with your heart that you believe and are justified, and it is with your mouth that you confess and are saved."

Romans 10:10

RECEIVING SALVATION

HOW TO MINISTER

Simple Steps To Salvation

1. Conviction of a sinful life is brought by the Holy Spirit. Every person without Jesus Christ is a sinner.

2. A person repents of sin and asks Jesus Christ to come into their heart, then confesses that they are born again.
    - Romans 10:10

("Prayer of Salvation" is found on the next page)

3. That person instantly becomes a new creation through the grace of God.
    - 2 Corinthians 5:17
    - Ephesians 2:8-9

4. Just as a newborn baby needs nourishment, exercise and love in order to grow – it is the same with a newborn Christian believer!
    - 1 Peter 2:2

RECEIVING SALVATION

HOW TO MINISTER

Simple "Prayer Of Salvation"

Ask the recipient to repeat this simple prayer following you:

"Father, forgive my sins.
Jesus come into my heart.
Make me the kind of person You want me to be.
Thank you for saving me."

Ask the person, "where is Jesus right now?" If they answer, "In my heart" say, "Congratulations on being a child of God! If their answer is anything other than, "In my heart," have them repeat the prayer after you again.

Encourage new believers to do the following:

- **Start reading the Holy Bible**

- **Find a friendly church that teaches God's Word.**

- **Spend time each day praying to God**

RECEIVING SALVATION

SCRIPTURES
OLD TESTAMENT:

Psalms 116:12-13
How can I repay the Lord for all His goodness to me? I will lift up the cup of salvation and call on the Name of the Lord.

Isaiah 12:2
Surely God is my salvation; I will trust and not be afraid. The Lord, the Lord, is my strength and my song; He has become my salvation.

Other Scriptures:
Romans 5:12
Ephesians 2:8-9
John 1:12

RECEIVING SALVATION

SCRIPTURES
NEW TESTAMENT:

John 3:16
For God so loved the world that He gave His one and only Son, that whoever believes in Him shall not perish but have eternal life.

John 3:7
You should not be surprised at My saying, You must be born again.

Romans 10:9-10
That if you confess with your mouth, "Jesus is Lord," and believe in your heart that God raised Him from the dead, you will be saved. For it is with your heart that you believe and are justified, and it is with your mouth that you confess and are saved.

RECEIVING SALVATION

<u>PRAYER</u>

Lord God, You gave Your only Son that if we would believe on Him we would be saved and have eternal life. *Repeat this prayer after me:* "Lord, I repent, am sorry for my sins and recognize I am in great need of You as my savior. Thank You for sending Jesus to die on the cross for my sins. I invite You now to become the Lord of my life, Jesus. I surrender control, receive You by faith and confess that You died and were raised from the grave for me. By the supernatural love and power of the precious Holy Spirit I declare that I am Yours and You are mine. I believe You have washed my sins in Your precious blood and I am new. The old has passed away and I am Your child. I need Your help in changing my mind, my attitude, my thoughts and the course of my life. I will trust in You and will not be afraid anymore. Thank You for loving me, saving me and setting me free. I will worship You and thank You for the new life you have given me today. I long to know more of Your infinite love. We pray and seal this salvation in Jesus' mighty Name, Amen."

FORGIVENESS

<u>SCRIPTURES</u>
OLD TESTAMENT:

Jeremiah 31:34
No longer will a man teach his neighbor, or a man his brother, saying, 'Know the Lord,' because they will all know Me, from the least of them to the greatest," declares the Lord. For I will forgive their wickedness and will remember their sins no more.

Jeremiah 31:37
This is what the Lord says: "Only if the heavens above can be measured and the foundations of the earth below be searched out will I reject all the descendants of Israel because of all they have done," declares the Lord.

Daniel 9:9
The Lord our God is merciful and forgiving, even though we have rebelled against Him.

FORGIVENESS

<u>SCRIPTURES</u>
NEW TESTAMENT:

Matthew 9:4-7
Knowing their thoughts, Jesus said, Why do you entertain evil thoughts in your hearts? Which is easier: to say, Your sins are forgiven, or to say, Get up and walk? But so that you may know that the Son of Man has authority on earth to forgive sins.... Then He said to the paralytic, Get up, take your mat and go home. And the man got up and went home.

Romans 4:6-8
David says the same thing when he speaks of the blessedness of the man to whom God credits righteousness apart from works: Blessed are they whose transgressions are forgiven, whose sins are covered. Blessed is the man whose sin the Lord will never count against him.

FORGIVENESS

<u>PRAYER</u>

Dear Lord Jesus, I come into agreement for _____ right now. He/she has repented and asked for Your love and forgiveness, Lord. Because You hear us when we pray we thank You for this work that has already begun. Forgive him/her for those situations and circumstances he/she is concerned about. I declare _____ is free from any guilt, condemnation or bondage as they receive Your forgiveness today. Teach him/her to forgive others as You have freely forgiven him/her. Even now You may be bringing people to their mind who they need to forgive, so I ask You to do a quick work in their heart. Teach them to keep short accounts of wrongs that have been done to them. Teach them to forgive quickly so as not to harbor offense in their heart, the place where Your Covenant is written. Renew their mind, Lord and replace any wrong thinking with a new Baptism of Your Spirit and the fruit He brings. Teach them that Your ways are holy and they are to be holy as You are holy. We thank You for forgiveness today and for a new beginning for _____, in the mighty Name of Jesus, Amen.

UNSAVED
LOVED ONES

<u>SCRIPTURES</u>
OLD TESTAMENT:

Deuteronomy 9:26

I prayed to the Lord and said, O Sovereign Lord, do not destroy Your people, Your own inheritance that You redeemed by Your great power and brought out of Egypt with a mighty hand.

Nehemiah 9:28

But as soon as they were at rest, they again did what was evil in your sight. Then You abandoned them to the hand of their enemies so that they ruled over them. And when they cried out to You again, You heard from heaven, and in Your compassion You delivered them time after time.

UNSAVED
LOVED ONES

SCRIPTURES
NEW TESTAMENT:

Acts 2:21
And everyone who calls on the Name of the Lord will be saved.

Luke 19:9
Jesus said to him, Today salvation has come to this house, because this man, too, is a son of Abraham.

1 Peter 3:1
Wives, in the same way be submissive to your husbands so that, if any of them do not believe the word, they may be won over without words by the behavior of their wives.

UNSAVED LOVED ONES

<u>PRAYER</u>

Father God, we stand in agreement for _____ and for their salvation. We know You love them, are mindful of their situation and hear us when we pray. Thank You for Your promise, Lord, that whosoever will call on the Name of Jesus will be saved and set free. We ask You now to draw _____ close to You. Cover this life with revelation and illumination that they need to repent and accept You as their savior and Lord. Help _____ to be a good witness and example of Your great love and remind him/her to thank You for _____'s salvation by faith. By Your grace and through faith we declare this answer is done, in the mighty Name of Jesus. We decree salvation has come to this person and to their household, even now as You are drawing them by Your love. Bring in the right people to share the truth of Your Word with them and remove all the wrong people from their life right now. We trust You in the freedom that You are bringing right now to this precious family, in Jesus Name, Amen.

HOLY
SPIRIT
& GLORY

"But you will receive power when the Holy Spirit comes on you; and you will be my witnesses…"

Acts 1:8

BAPTISM IN THE SPIRIT

SCRIPTURES
OLD TESTAMENT:

Isaiah 11:2

The Spirit of the Lord will rest on Him—the Spirit of wisdom and of understanding, the Spirit of counsel and of power, the Spirit of knowledge and of the fear of the Lord.

Zechariah 12:10

And I will pour out on the house of David and the inhabitants of Jerusalem a spirit of grace and supplication. They will look on Me, the One they have pierced, and they will mourn for Him as one mourns for an only child, and grieve bitterly for him as one grieves for a firstborn son.

BAPTISM IN THE SPIRIT

SCRIPTURES
NEW TESTAMENT:

Ephesians 5:18-20
Do not get drunk on wine, which leads to debauchery. Instead, be filled with the Spirit. Speak to one another with psalms, hymns and spiritual songs. Sing and make music in your heart to the Lord, always giving thanks to God the Father for everything, in the Name of our Lord Jesus Christ.

Acts 13:52
And the disciples were filled with joy and with the Holy Spirit.

Matthew 3:11
I baptize you with water for repentance. But after me will come One who is more powerful than I, whose sandals I am not fit to carry. He will baptize you with the Holy Spirit and with fire.

BAPTISM IN THE SPIRIT

PRAYER

Precious Lord, thank You for _____ and his/her hunger to be filled with Your Spirit. You promised to give Him to those who ask You, so I ask You to fill _____ with Your Spirit right now, Lord. By faith I declare he/she is being filled now with the evidence of speaking in tongues. I pray he/she is receiving the fullness of Your Spirit as the power of God now rests upon them. Thank You for the miracle of the supernatural power of God that is with them now and this empowerment will enable them to walk with the Comforter. The life and power of Jesus now dwells within them and we can come to You with thanks and great anticipation of what You're going to do in their life. I pray for newness of life, new beginnings and creative ideas that come straight from heaven for _____. Thank You for the convicting and transforming power of Holy Spirit that is already at work in their life. Help him/her to follow Your voice and Your leading with evidence of great peace and assurance. Thank You for the Spirit of truth that dwells within them now and we worship You together for this mighty wonder! In Jesus' Name we pray, Amen.

WALKING IN
THE GLORY REALM

<u>SCRIPTURES</u>
OLD TESTAMENT:

Joel 2:28
And afterward, I will pour out My Spirit on all people. Your sons and daughters will prophesy, your old men will dream dreams, your young men will see visions.

Leviticus 20:26
You are to be holy to Me because I, the Lord, am holy, and I have set you apart from the nations to be My own.

Deuteronomy 28:9
The Lord will establish you as His holy people, as He promised you on oath, if you keep the commands of the Lord Your God and walk in His ways.

WALKING IN
THE GLORY REALM

SCRIPTURES
NEW TESTAMENT:

Romans 8:1-2
Therefore, there is now no condemnation for those who are in Christ Jesus, because through Christ Jesus the law of the Spirit of life set me free from the law of sin and death.

Galatians 5:16-17
So I say, live by the Spirit, and you will not gratify the desires of the sinful nature. For the sinful nature desires what is contrary to the Spirit, and the Spirit what is contrary to the sinful nature. They are in conflict with each other, so that you do not do what you want.

WALKING IN THE GLORY REALM

<u>PRAYER</u>

Dear Lord, thank You for filling _____ with the precious Holy Spirit of Glory. What an honor it is to walk in the Glory Realm. I pray right now for _____ to be filled a fresh with the power of the Spirit, enabling them to walk forth in the fullness of Your love, power and authority. As he/she has chosen to crucify their flesh and walk in the Spirit, I ask for Your help, guidance and wisdom. Lead and guide them into all Truth so they can worship You with pure hearts of flesh. Give them a hunger for Your Word, Your righteousness and Your holiness that they would grow quickly in the things of the Spirit. Holy Spirit, speak to them clearly about turning from deception, wrong relationships and any wrong direction. May their life be an example to others of the great unlimited love You have for them and use them mightily for Your glory. Holy Spirit, I ask You to help them press forward into the mark of the high calling in Christ Jesus. We thank You for the great things You are doing in this precious life, in Jesus' Name. Amen.

FAITH

<u>SCRIPTURES</u>
OLD TESTAMENT:

Habakkuk 2:4
See, he is puffed up; his desires are not upright, but the righteous will live by his faith.

Psalms 37:3
Trust in the Lord and do good; dwell in the land and enjoy safe pasture.

FAITH

<u>SCRIPTURES</u>
NEW TESTAMENT:

Hebrews 11:1, 6
Now faith is being sure of what we hope for and certain of what we do not see. And without faith it is impossible to please God, because anyone who comes to Him must believe that He exists and that He rewards those who earnestly seek Him.

James 2:18
But someone will say, You have faith; I have deeds. Show me your faith without deeds, and I will show you my faith by what I do.

Galatians 3:9
So those who have faith are blessed along with Abraham, the man of faith.

FAITH

PRAYER

Dear Lord, You said in Your Word that the just would live by faith and without faith it is impossible to please You. Father, _____ desires to please You in their walk with You and is asking for a greater measure of Your faith. Increase their faith right now, flood them with Your faith, overtake them with faith, Holy Spirit. They will no longer doubt, no longer be tossed to and fro by every wind of doctrine, or by every opinion of those closest to them. They will know the truth and it will set them free to soar to greater heights in faith. Teach them to believe for the impossible, do the unimaginable and see great miracles, signs and wonders. Holy Spirit, remove double-mindedness and unbelief. When tests and trials come help them to focus on You, Lord and believe that You will carry them through on the wings of Your love. Keep him/her steadfast in their faith and growing in the knowledge of Your love and faithfulness in their life. You will never leave them or forsake them and we thank You for that, Father. In Jesus' Name we pray, Amen.

VISIONS & DREAMS

SCRIPTURES
OLD TESTAMENT:

Numbers 12:5-6
Then the Lord came down in a pillar of cloud; he stood at the entrance to the Tent and summoned Aaron and Miriam. When both of them stepped forward, he said, "Listen to my words: "When a prophet of the Lord is among you, I reveal myself to him in visions, I speak to him in dreams.

Job 33:14-16
For God does speak—now one way, now another — though man may not perceive it. In a dream, in a vision of the night, when deep sleep falls on men as they slumber in their beds, he may speak in their ears and terrify them with warnings.

VISIONS & DREAMS

<u>SCRIPTURES</u>
NEW TESTAMENT:

Acts 2:17-18
"In the last days, God says, I will pour out my Spirit on all people. Your sons and daughters will prophesy, your young men will see visions, your old men will dream dreams. Even on my servants, both men and women, I will pour out my Spirit in those days, and they will prophesy..."

Colossians 3:2
Set your minds on things above, not on earthly things.

Hebrews 11:27
By faith he left Egypt, not fearing the king's anger; he persevered because he saw him who is invisible.

EMPOWERMENT

SCRIPTURES
OLD TESTAMENT:

Deuteronomy 28:12
The Lord will open the heavens, the storehouse of His bounty, to send rain on your land in season and to bless all the work of your hands. You will lend to many nations but will borrow from none.

Joshua 1:6
Be strong and courageous, because you will lead these people to inherit the land I swore to their forefathers to give them.

Psalms 68:35
You are awesome, O God, in your sanctuary; the God of Israel gives power and strength to His people. Praise be to God!

EMPOWERMENT

SCRIPTURES
NEW TESTAMENT:

Matthew 9:37-38
Then He said to His disciples, The harvest is plentiful but the workers are few. Ask the Lord of the harvest, therefore, to send out workers into His harvest field.

Psalms 68:35
You are awesome, O God, in your sanctuary; the God of Israel gives power and strength to His people. Praise be to God!

EMPOWERMENT

PRAYER

Holy Spirit, thank You for _____ and the call You have on his/her life. I thank You right now for empowering him/her to the work You have called him/her to do. I thank You for the power of precious Holy Spirit that resides on the inside of him/her. I thank You for the release of a great flow of power and anointing that will increase wise decisions and cause great testimonies to come forth. You are granting to them today according to the riches of Your glory, power and strength in their inner man, in their spirit, in their mind. You are doing marvelous things in this life even now, Lord and causing them to have hinds' feet so they will be able to walk in and among the high places of Your glory. Infuse their very being with Your presence and empowering glory and cause them to mount up on the wings of eagles and soar to greater heights of faith. There is nothing You cannot do with this life, Lord as their eyes of faith remain fixed and focused on You. We thank You for this empowerment today and thank You for the release of Your glory from head to toe. Thank You, God, in Jesus' Name we pray, Amen.

ANOINTING

<u>SCRIPTURES</u>
OLD TESTAMENT:

Daniel 4:17
The decision is announced by messengers, the holy ones declare the verdict, so that the living may know that the Most High is sovereign over the kingdoms of men and gives them to anyone He wishes and sets over them the lowliest of men.

1 Samuel 16:12b
Then the Lord said, Rise and anoint him; he is the one.

Isaiah 61:1
The Spirit of the Sovereign Lord is on me, because the Lord has anointed me to preach good news to the poor. He has sent me to bind up the brokenhearted, to proclaim freedom for the captives and release from darkness for the prisoners.

ANOINTING

SCRIPTURES
NEW TESTAMENT:

Matthew 9:37-38
Then He said to His disciples, The harvest is plentiful but the workers are few. Ask the Lord of the harvest, therefore, to send out workers into His harvest field.

Luke 4:18-19
The Spirit of the Lord is on me, because He has anointed me to preach good news to the poor. He has sent me to proclaim freedom for the prisoners and recovery of sight for the blind, to release the oppressed, to proclaim the year of the Lord's favor.

ANOINTING

<u>PRAYER</u>

Father God, as You anointed Jesus of Nazareth to be King in heaven and earth and reign with You in glory, and as You even anointed David to be king, prophet and priest, I ask You to anoint _____ by the power of Holy Spirit to the work You have called him/her to do. As Jesus was anointed here on this earth, so shall we be anointed, Lord, so I thank You right now for the anointing that You are releasing today. I thank You for _____ and the wondrous plan You have. Even if he/she has only seen glimpses of that plan, bring revelation and illumination. Open doors of opportunities for his/her to be a blessing and to bring life to others, Father. Anointed by the Holy Spirit and in agreement with You Lord, there are no limits of what You can do with this life. Surrendered and submitted to Your Spirit, I declare mighty works will they do in Your Name, Father. Fill them to overflowing with Your Spirit and baptize them with fire as they defeat the works of darkness and open the doors to the prisoners. We thank You for the mighty anointing that now rests on _____ and we pray in Jesus' lovely Name, Amen.

SIGNS & WONDERS

<u>SCRIPTURES</u>
OLD TESTAMENT:

Daniel 4:2
It is my pleasure to tell you about the miraculous signs and wonders that the Most High God has performed for me.

Daniel 6:27
He rescues and he saves; he performs signs and wonders in the heavens and on the earth.

Isaiah 8:18
Behold, I and the children whom the Lord hath given me are for signs and for wonders in Israel from the Lord of hosts, which dwelleth in mount Zion. (KJV)

SIGNS & WONDERS

SCRIPTURES
NEW TESTAMENT:

Acts 5:12,14
The apostles performed many miraculous signs and wonders among the people... Nevertheless, more and more men and women believed in the Lord and were added to their number.

Mark 16:17-20
And these signs will accompany those who believe: In my name they will drive out demons; they will speak in new tongues; they will pick up snakes with their hands; and when they drink deadly poison, it will not hurt them at all; they will place their hands on sick people, and they will get well." After the Lord Jesus had spoken to them, he was taken up into heaven and he sat at the right hand of God. Then the disciples went out and preached everywhere, and the Lord worked with them and confirmed his word by the signs that accompanied it.

BREAKER ANOINTING

SCRIPTURES
OLD TESTAMENT:

Micah 2:13
One who breaks open the way will go up before them; they will break through the gate and go out. Their king will pass through before them, the Lord at their head."

Isaiah 10:27
And it shall come to pass in that day, that his burden shall be taken away from off thy shoulder, and his yoke from off thy neck, and the yoke shall be destroyed because of the anointing. (KJV)

Isaiah 52:9
Break forth into joy, sing together, ye waste places of Jerusalem: for the Lord hath comforted his people, he hath redeemed Jerusalem. (KJV)

BREAKER ANOINTING

<u>SCRIPTURES</u>
NEW TESTAMENT:

Matthew 11:12
From the days of John the Baptist until now, the kingdom of heaven has been forcefully advancing, and forceful men lay hold of it.

Luke 4:18
The Spirit of the Lord is on me, because he has anointed me to preach good news to the poor. He has sent me to proclaim freedom for the prisoners and recovery of sight for the blind, to release the oppressed.

BREAKER ANOINTING

<u>PRAYER</u>

Dear Father, in the name of Jesus, I thank you for releasing a breaker anointing upon _____ by the power of Your Holy Spirit.

I declare that this supernatural breaker anointing from heaven will shake every shackle loose that has been holding back individuals, churches, ministries, cities and nations from coming into their destiny and full inheritance.

I thank you Lord that as my brother/sister is released into this breaker anointing that you will use them in a powerful and mighty way to proclaim your gospel.

Right now, I speak forth the joy of the Lord that will be your strength and enable you to go with this breaker anointing. All sadness and hardship must go right now as you are breaking forth into joy right now!

Thank you Lord for releasing great breakthroughs in all areas of _____'s life in the mighty name of Jesus Christ. Amen.

RELEASING ANGELS

<u>SCRIPTURES</u>
OLD TESTAMENT:

Psalm 34:7
The angel of the Lord encamps around those who fear him, and he delivers them.

Daniel 6:21-22
Daniel answered, "O king, live forever! My God sent his angel, and he shut the mouths of the lions. They have not hurt me, because I was found innocent in his sight. Nor have I ever done any wrong before you, O king."

RELEASING ANGELS

SCRIPTURES
NEW TESTAMENT:

Matthew 24:31
And he will send his angels with a loud trumpet call, and they will gather his elect from the four winds, from one end of the heavens to the other.

Hebrews 1:13-14
To which of the angels did God ever say, "Sit at my right hand until I make your enemies a footstool for your feet"? Are not all angels ministering spirits sent to serve those who will inherit salvation?

Hebrews 13:2
Do not forget to entertain strangers, for by so doing some people have entertained angels without knowing it.

OPEN HEAVENS

<u>SCRIPTURES</u>
OLD TESTAMENT:

Ezekiel 1:1
In the thirtieth year, in the fourth month on the fifth day, while I was among the exiles by the Kebar River, the heavens were opened and I saw visions of God.

Deuteronomy 28:12
The Lord will open the heavens, the storehouse of his bounty, to send rain on your land in season and to bless all the work of your hands. You will lend to many nations but will borrow from none.

Isaiah 64:1-2
Oh, that you would rend the heavens and come down, that the mountains would tremble before you! As when fire sets twigs ablaze and causes water to boil, come down to make your name known to your enemies and cause the nations to quake before you!

OPEN HEAVENS

SCRIPTURES
NEW TESTAMENT:

Matthew 3:16-17
As soon as Jesus was baptized, he went up out of the water. At that moment heaven was opened, and he saw the Spirit of God descending like a dove and lighting on him. And a voice from heaven said, "This is my Son, whom I love; with him I am well pleased."

Acts 10:9-11
...Peter went up on the roof to pray. He became hungry and wanted something to eat, and while the meal was being prepared, he fell into a trance. He saw heaven opened and something like a large sheet being let down to earth by its four corners.

Revelation 19:11
I saw heaven standing open and there before me was a white horse, whose rider is called Faithful and True.

IMPARTATION

<u>SCRIPTURES</u>
OLD TESTAMENT:

Isaiah 49:8
This is what the Lord says: In the time of My favor I will answer you, and in the day of salvation I will help you; I will keep you and will make you to be a covenant for the people, to restore the land and to reassign its desolate inheritances.

Deuteronomy 28:9-10
The Lord will establish you as His holy people, as He promised you on oath, if you keep the commands of the Lord your God and walk in His ways. Then all the peoples on earth will see that you are called by the Name of the Lord, and they will fear you.

IMPARTATION

<u>SCRIPTURES</u>
NEW TESTAMENT:

John 13:34-35

A new command I give you: love one another as I have loved you so you must love one another. By this all men will know that you are My disciples, if you love one another.

Matthew 28:18-20

Then Jesus came to them and said, All authority in heaven and on earth has been given to Me. Therefore go and make disciples of all nations, baptizing them in the Name of the Father and of the Son and of the Holy Spirit, and teaching them to obey everything I have commanded you. And surely I am with you always, to the very end of the age.

IMPARTATION

<u>PRAYER</u>

Holy Spirit, thank You for _____'s life and hunger for greater impartation of Your power and authority in their life. Father, we thank You for everything that You have is available to them. Everything You are is available to those who ask by the power of Holy Spirit. We ask right now that You fill _____ with a powerful impartation of wisdom, strength and supernatural ability to preach, teach, prophesy, testify and declare the works of the Lord! Impart revelation knowledge, greater discernment, everything that he/she needs to live a life of godliness, holiness and supernatural wisdom unto You, Father. All authority in heaven and on earth has been given to them, from You, Jesus. Your disciples will go where You have called them, baptize people in the Name of the Father and of the Son and of the Holy Spirit, teaching them to obey everything You said in Your Word. Thank You for this special time of impartation, Holy Spirit. Thank You for the hunger and thirst _____ has shown; the tremendous passion for Your Word and to carry the message of the Gospel. Thank You, Father, in Jesus Name I pray, Amen.

LIFE ISSUES

"I am come that they might have life, and that they might have it more abundantly."

John 10:10

A NATION AND ITS LEADERS

SCRIPTURES
OLD TESTAMENT:

Exodus 19:6

You will be for me a kingdom of priests and a holy nation. These are the words you are to speak to the Israelites.

Exodus 34:10

Then the Lord said: I am making a covenant with you. Before all your people I will do wonders never before done in any nation in all the world. The people you live among will see how awesome is the work that I, the Lord, will do for you.

Jeremiah 29:7

Also, seek the peace and prosperity of the city to which I have carried you into exile. Pray to the Lord for it, because if it prospers, you too will prosper.

A NATION AND ITS LEADERS

SCRIPTURES
NEW TESTAMENT:

Luke 24:47
And repentance and forgiveness of sins will be preached in His Name to all nations, beginning at Jerusalem.

1Timothy 2:1-2
I urge, then, first of all, that requests, prayers, intercession and thanksgiving be made for everyone—for kings and all those in authority, that we may live peaceful and quiet lives in all godliness and holiness.

Revelation 22:2
On each side of the river stood the tree of life, bearing twelve crops of fruit, yielding its fruit every month. And the leaves of the tree are for the healing of the nations.

A NATION AND ITS LEADERS

PRAYER

Father God, I stand in agreement with _____ for the nation of _____ (or the world). I thank You for the leaders there and pray for a move of God's Spirit over all those in authority, in government, in the schools, legal systems, churches, media and all other positions of great influence. Holy Spirit we ask that all the people of God throughout this land will humble themselves and pray and seek Your face and turn from their wicked ways. Then You will hear from heaven and will forgive their sins and heal their land. Holy Spirit, bring the truth of God's Word to this land. Open the door to the gospel to leaders who are not saved. Bring the power of Holy Spirit and salvation to the nation of _____, Lord. May fire from heaven fall and burn up that which is not of You, Lord. Pour out Your Holy Spirit on the families of this nation; bring children back to their parents and restore marriages that have been broken, Father. May the knowledge of Your glory cover the earth as the waters cover the seas. We trust You and believe You are doing it now. In Jesus' mighty Name we pray, Amen.

ATTITUDE

<u>SCRIPTURES</u>
OLD TESTAMENT:

Proverbs 15:13
A happy heart makes the face cheerful, but heartache crushes the spirit.

Proverbs 17:22
A cheerful heart is good medicine, but a crushed spirit dries up the bones.

Proverbs 31:26
She openeth her mouth with wisdom; and in her tongue is the law of kindness.

Daniel 6:3
Then this Daniel was preferred above the presidents and princes, because an excellent spirit was in him; and the king thought to set him over the whole realm.

ATTITUDE

SCRIPTURES
NEW TESTAMENT:

Matthew 12:34-35
For out of the overflow of the heart the mouth speaks. The good man brings good things out of the good stored up in him, and the evil man brings evil things out of the evil stored up in him.

Ephesians 4:22
You were taught, with regard to your former way of life, to put off your old self, which is being corrupted by its deceitful desires.

Philippians 2:5
Your attitude should be the same as that of Christ Jesus.

CREATIVITY

<u>SCRIPTURES</u>
OLD TESTAMENT:

Psalm 139:14-15
I praise you because I am fearfully and wonderfully made; your works are wonderful, I know that full well. My frame was not hidden from you when I was made in the secret place. When I was woven together in the depths of the earth.

Proverbs 8:12
I wisdom dwell with prudence, and find out knowledge of witty inventions.

Isaiah 43:19
See, I am doing a new thing! Now it springs up; do you not perceive it?

CREATIVITY

<u>SCRIPTURES</u>
NEW TESTAMENT:

Romans 8:19-21
The creation waits in eager expectation for the sons of God to be revealed. For the creation was subjected to frustration, not by its own choice, but by the will of the one who subjected it, in hope that the creation itself will be liberated from its bondage to decay and brought into the glorious freedom of the children of God.

Colossians 1:15
He is the image of the invisible God, the firstborn over all creation.

1 Corinthians 4:16
Therefore I urge you to imitate me.

DESIRES

<u>SCRIPTURES</u>
OLD TESTAMENT:

Psalm 37:4
Delight yourself in the Lord and he will give you the desires of your heart.

Psalm 38:9
All my longings lie open before you, O Lord; my sighing is not hidden from you.

Proverbs 10:24
What the wicked dreads will overtake him; what the righteous desire will be granted.

Proverbs 13:12,19
Hope deferred makes the heart sick, but a longing fulfilled is a tree of life. A longing fulfilled is sweet to the soul...

DESIRES

<u>SCRIPTURES</u>
NEW TESTAMENT:

Mark 11:24
Therefore I say unto you, What things soever ye desire, when ye pray, believe that ye receive them, and ye shall have them.

1 John 3:22
And whatsoever we ask, we receive of him, because we keep his commandments, and do those things that are pleasing in his sight.

1 John 5:15
And if we know that he hear us, whatsoever we ask, we know that we have the petitions that we desired of him.

RESTORATION OF TIME

SCRIPTURES
OLD TESTAMENT:

Job 33:4

The Spirit of God has made me; the breath of the Almighty gives me life.

Proverbs 9:10-11

The fear of the Lord is the beginning of wisdom, and knowledge of the Holy One is understanding. For through me your days will be many, and years will be added to your life.

Joel 2:25

And I will restore to you the years that the locust hath eaten...

Other Scriptures:
Exodus 9:5
Joshua 10:12-14
Colossians 4:5

RESTORATION OF TIME

<u>SCRIPTURES</u>
NEW TESTAMENT:

Matthew 12:13
Then saith he to the man, Stretch forth thine hand. And he stretched it forth; and it was restored whole, like as the other.

Philippians 3:13-14
Brethren, I count not myself to have apprehended: but this one thing I do, forgetting those things which are behind, and reaching forth unto those things which are before, I press toward the mark for the prize of the high calling of God in Christ Jesus.

Ephesians 5:15-16
See then that ye walk circumspectly, not as fools, but as wise, Redeeming the time, because the days are evil.

ROMANCE

<u>SCRIPTURES</u>
OLD TESTAMENT:

Proverbs 15:17

Better a meal of vegetables where there is love than a fattened calf with hatred.

Ecclesiastes 4:9

Two are better than one, because they have a good return for their work.

Song of Solomon 1:4

Take me away with you—let us hurry! Let the king bring me into his chambers. We rejoice and delight in you; we will praise your love more than wine. How right they are to adore you!

ROMANCE

<u>SCRIPTURES</u>
NEW TESTAMENT:

1 Corinthians 13:4-6
Love is patient, love is kind. It does not envy, it does not boast, it is not proud. It is not rude, it is not self-seeking, it is not easily angered, it keeps no record of wrongs. Love does not delight in evil but rejoices with the truth. It always protects, always trusts, always hopes, always perseveres.

Ephesians 5:25
Husbands, love your wives, just as Christ loved the church and gave himself up for her.

LOSING A LOVED ONE

<u>SCRIPTURES</u>
OLD TESTAMENT:

Isaiah 61:3
And provide for those who grieve in Zion, to bestow on them a crown of beauty instead of ashes, the oil of gladness instead of mourning, and a garment of praise instead of a spirit of despair. They will be called oaks of righteousness, a planting of the Lord for the display of His splendor.

Psalms 23:4
Even though I walk through the valley of the shadow of death, I will fear no evil, for You are with me; Your rod and Your staff, they comfort me.

LOSING A LOVED ONE

<u>SCRIPTURES</u>
NEW TESTAMENT:

2 Corinthians 5:17
Therefore, if anyone is in Christ, he is a new creation; the old has gone, the new has come!

John 16:20
I tell you the truth, you will weep and mourn while the world rejoices. You will grieve, but your grief will turn to joy.

1 Thessalonians 4:13
Brothers, we do not want you to be ignorant about those who fall asleep, or to grieve like the rest of men, who have no hope. We believe that Jesus died and rose again and so we believe that God will bring with Jesus those who have fallen asleep in Him.

LOSING A LOVED ONE

<u>PRAYER</u>

Holy Spirit, You are the great Comforter and we thank You Lord for comforting us in times of need. I come to You on behalf of _____. In the Name that is above every Name in the heavens and on earth, Jesus Christ, I ask You to pour out Your supernatural Comfort right now. Impart hope and healing to this hurting heart right now, Jesus. Let the mourning be turned to joy as he/she senses Your great love for him/her and that You know the feelings of loss and pain. I ask You to bring peace now where there is sorrow and healing where there is pain. Fill the void Lord Jesus with Your love and help him/her to rejoice in knowing that all things work together for good to those who love You, Lord. Thank You, Holy Spirit, for allowing us to see Your glory and experience Your mighty love. We are forever grateful Holy Spirit for Your supernatural Comfort that You have imparted today. We lift our eyes unto You, Jesus, the author and finisher of our faith. We praise You and worship You that we will see our loved ones again very soon. We pray in the matchless Name above all names, Jesus. Amen.

SINGLE BELIEVER DESIRING MARRIAGE

SCRIPTURES
OLD TESTAMENT:

Psalms 37:4-5
Delight yourself in the Lord and He will give you the desires of your heart. Commit your way to the Lord; trust in Him and He will do this.

Psalms 9:10
Those who know Your Name will trust in You, for You, Lord, have never forsaken those who seek You.

Psalms 68:6
God sets the lonely in families, He leads forth the prisoners with singing; but the rebellious live in a sun-scorched land.

SINGLE BELIEVER DESIRING MARRIAGE

SCRIPTURES
NEW TESTAMENT:

2 Corinthians 1:20
For no matter how many promises God has made, they are "Yes" in Christ. And so through him the "Amen" is spoken by us to the glory of God.

John 16:23-24
In that day you will no longer ask me anything. I tell you the truth, My Father will give you whatever you ask in My Name. Until now you have not asked for anything in My Name. Ask and you will receive, and your joy will be complete.

SINGLE BELIEVER DESIRING MARRIAGE

<u>PRAYER</u>

Dear Father, I stand in agreement with _____ for his/her hearts' desires to be married. I ask that Your Holy Spirit will prepare his/her heart to be the perfect helpmate for their spouse. I ask that You guide them and instruct them specifically in the areas that would compliment the special one You are bringing to them. I pray for patience and endurance in the preparation, God, and that they will run and not grow weary. Help him/her to trust You with all their heart and acknowledge You in all their ways as You direct their path. I break all soul ties with relationships from the past in Jesus' Name and ask You to set them free this day to follow Your path and Your will by Your Spirit. May the spouse have full confidence in them lacking nothing of great value. May they bring the spouse good and not harm all the days of his/her life. Fill them with hope, joy and faith in knowing that You have provided all good things for Your glory. We praise You and thank You that You are doing what You promised. In Jesus' Name we pray, Amen.

INTEGRITY

SCRIPTURES
OLD TESTAMENT:

Psalm 112:5
Good will come to him who is generous and lends freely, who conducts his affairs with justice.

Proverbs 10:9
The man of integrity walks securely, but he who takes crooked paths will be found out.

Proverbs 12:22
The Lord detests lying lips, but he delights in men who are truthful.

Proverbs 20:7
The righteous man leads a blameless life; blessed are his children after him.

NEW WINE INTERNATIONAL
INTEGRITY

<u>SCRIPTURES</u>
NEW TESTAMENT:

2 Timothy 4:18
The Lord will rescue me from every evil attack and will bring me safely to his heavenly kingdom. To him be glory for ever and ever. Amen.

Philippians 2:3-4
Do nothing out of selfish ambition or vain conceit, but in humility consider others better than yourselves. Each of you should look not only to your own interests, but also to the interests of others.

Luke 12:48
But the one who does not know and does things deserving punishment will be beaten with few blows. From everyone who has been given much, much will be demanded; and from the one who has been entrusted with much, much more will be asked.

WISDOM

<u>SCRIPTURES</u>
OLD TESTAMENT:

Psalm 51:6
Surely you desire truth in the inner parts you teach me wisdom in the inmost place.

Psalm 90:12
Teach us to number our days aright, that we may gain a heart of wisdom.

Proverbs 2:6
For the Lord gives wisdom, and from his mouth come knowledge and understanding.

Ecclesiastes 7:12
Wisdom is a shelter as money is a shelter, but the advantage of knowledge is this: that wisdom preserves the life of its possessor.

WISDOM

<u>SCRIPTURES</u>
NEW TESTAMENT:

James 1:5
If any of you lacks wisdom, he should ask God, who gives generously to all without finding fault, and it will be given to him.

James 3:17
But the wisdom that comes from heaven is first of all pure; then peace-loving, considerate, submissive, full of mercy and good fruit, impartial and sincere.

Romans 11:33
Oh, the depth of the riches of the wisdom and knowledge of God! How unsearchable his judgments, and his paths beyond tracing out!

FINANCES

"...Let the Lord be magnified, Who takes pleasure in the prosperity of His servant."

Psalm 35:27

DAILY PROVISION

<u>SCRIPTURES</u>
OLD TESTAMENT:

Psalms 37:25
I was young and now I am old, yet I have never seen the righteous forsaken or their children begging bread.

Deuteronomy 28:11
The Lord will grant you abundant prosperity—in the fruit of your womb, the young of your livestock and the crops of your ground—in the land He swore to your forefathers to give you.

Haggai 2:8
The silver is Mine and the gold is Mine, declares the Lord Almighty.

DAILY PROVISION

<u>SCRIPTURES</u>
NEW TESTAMENT:

Luke 11:3
Give us each day our daily bread.

Philippians 4:19
And my God will meet all your needs according to His glorious riches in Christ Jesus.

DAILY PROVISION

<u>PRAYER</u>

Jesus, we praise You and thank You for the rich blessings in our lives and _____ and I thank You for provision for his/her daily needs. You are the God of more than enough and we trust You, Jesus, with the needs that are represented here today. Impart Your supernatural faith and trust to _____ right now. Remove all fear and doubt as he/she believes You are the great provider. You are bringing even now all that is needed as he/she commits his/her life and his/her daily needs into Your hands. You are mindful of everything, Lord, even the lilies and grass in the fields. You came and You died so that _____ would have abundant spiritual and physical life so we trust You today. We thank You that You are working everything out for his/her good because he/she loves You, Lord. I thank You right now that You are El Shaddai, the God of more than enough. Pour out so much more that they would give to the needy as often as they want! We praise You and thank You that _____ is not going to be without. In the matchless Name of Jesus Christ we pray, Amen.

DIVINE CANCELLATION OF DEBT

<u>SCRIPTURES</u>
OLD TESTAMENT:

Numbers 30:2
When a man makes a vow to the Lord or takes an oath to obligate himself by a pledge, he must not break his word but must do everything he said.

Proverbs 6:1-5
My son, if you have put up security for your neighbor, if you have struck hands in pledge for another, if you have been trapped by what you said, ensnared by the words of your mouth, then do this, my son, to free yourself, since you have fallen into your neighbor's hands: Go and humble yourself; press your plea with your neighbor! Allow no sleep to your eyes, no slumber to your eyelids. Free yourself, like a gazelle from the hand of the hunter, like a bird from the snare of the fowler.

DIVINE CANCELLATION OF DEBT

SCRIPTURES
NEW TESTAMENT:

Hebrews 10:34-36
You sympathized with those in prison and joyfully accepted the confiscation of your property, because you knew that you yourselves had better and lasting possessions. So do not throw away your confidence; it will be richly rewarded. You need to persevere so that when you have done the will of God, you will receive what he has promised.

Other Scriptures:
Psalm 37:12-27
Jeremiah 33:7-9

DIVINE CANCELLATION OF DEBT

PRAYER

Dear Father, in the name of Jesus, I thank you for helping _____ to pay back debts that he/she owes.

Dear Lord, I ask for the supernatural power of Your Holy Spirit to intervene in this situation. As _____ labors to make things right, I thank you that you cause a divine flow of heavenly favor and blessing to overtake this situation.

I thank you that any loan, mortgage, credit card payment, bill that is past due, or other financial debt would be touched by the power of Your glory realm right now in the name of Jesus Christ.

We declare supernatural miracles and divine cancellation of this debt in Jesus name!

EMPLOYMENT

SCRIPTURES
OLD TESTAMENT:

Job 1:10
Have you not put a hedge around him and his household and everything he has? You have blessed the work of his hands, so that his flocks and herds are spread throughout the land.

Proverbs 10:4
Lazy hands make a man poor, but diligent hands bring wealth.

Deuteronomy 28:12
The Lord will open the heavens, the storehouse of His bounty, to send rain on your land in season and to bless all the work of your hands.

EMPLOYMENT

SCRIPTURES
NEW TESTAMENT:

Matthew 20:1-7
The Kingdom of heaven is like a landowner who went out early in the morning to hire men to work in his vineyard. He agreed to pay them a denarius for the day and sent them into his Vineyard. About the third hour he went out and saw others standing in the marketplace doing nothing. He told them, you also go and work in my vineyard, and I will pay you whatever is right. So they went. He went out again about the sixth hour and the ninth hour and did the same thing. About the eleventh hour he went out and found still others standing around. He asked them, why have you been standing here all day long doing nothing? Because no one has hired us, they answered. He said to them, you also go and work in my vineyard.

EMPLOYMENT

<u>PRAYER</u>

Father God, I lift up _____ and this job situation that concerns him/her right now. You said to cast all our cares on You, Father, so we cast this on You today. I ask You to lift the load and the burden from off these shoulders. Strengthen him/her and give him/her confidence that You are working all things for his/her good. I call down the exact employment opportunity from the heavenly realms right now in Jesus' mighty Name and declare it is done. Let patience have its perfect work, Lord until the right door manifests. I thank You for supernatural faith, and that _____ does not doubt that You have covered him/her in Your heavenly provision. Help him/her to trust You completely and lean not unto his/her own understanding but to acknowledge You in all his/her ways and You will direct his/her paths. May he/she worship, praise and thank You as he/she follows Your leading in where You want him/her to walk each day. There will be no lack in _____'s life. We thank You for employment, for provision and for an overflowing of Your Spirit, in Jesus' Name, Amen.

TITHES

<u>SCRIPTURES</u>
OLD TESTAMENT:

Genesis 14:19-20
And he blessed Abram, saying, Blessed be Abram by God Most High, Creator of heaven and earth. And blessed be God Most High, who delivered your enemies into your hand. Then Abram gave him a tenth of everything.

Malachi 3:10
Bring the whole tithe into the storehouse, that there may be food in My house. Test Me in this, says the Lord Almighty, and see if I will not throw open the floodgates of heaven and pour out so much blessing that you will not have room enough for it.

TITHES

<u>SCRIPTURES</u>
NEW TESTAMENT:

Romans 4:13

It was not through law that Abraham and his offspring received the promise that he would be heir of the world, but through the righteousness that comes by faith.

Matthew 23:23

Woe to you, teachers of the law and Pharisees, you hypocrites! You give a tenth of your spices—mint, dill and cumin. But you have neglected the more important matters of the law—justice, mercy and faithfulness. You should have practiced the latter, without neglecting the former.

TITHES

PRAYER

Father God, we thank You right now for the truth of Your Word. Your Word says we are to bring in the tithes to the storehouse that there would be food in Your house. I lift up _____ to You, Father and I ask You to work obedience in his/her heart concerning the tithe. We know tithing is Your commandment, to give 10% of our increase and trust You with our finances. If there is any fear in _____'s life, I renounce it right now in Jesus' Name. Release the blessing of Abraham over him/her right now for their faithful tithing. Everything they have belongs to You, even their increase so I pray he/she will give their tithe to the work of the Lord with joy knowing that a spiritual principal is being followed. Trusting fully in Your Word, Lord, we can obey without questioning because Your Word is true and we will receive a harvest from our obedience. Thank You for new freedom for _____ today, new blessings, greater faith and obedience in their life. I pray blessings on the place where he/she tithes and for spiritual food in abundance, more than he/she could ask or imagine, in Jesus' Name, Amen.

271

OFFERINGS

<u>SCRIPTURES</u>
OLD TESTAMENT:

Exodus 36:3

They received from Moses all the offerings the Israelites had brought to carry out the work of constructing the sanctuary. And the people continued to bring freewill offerings morning after morning.

Numbers 18:28

In this way you also will present an offering to the Lord from all the tithes you receive from the Israelites. From these tithes you must give the Lord's portion to Aaron the priest.

OFFERINGS

SCRIPTURES
NEW TESTAMENT:

Luke 6:38
Give, and it will be given to you. A good measure, pressed down, shaken together and running over, will be poured into your lap. For with the measure you use, it will be measured to you.

Hebrews 11:4
By faith Abel offered God a better sacrifice than Cain did. By faith he was commended as a righteous man, when God spoke well of his offerings. And by faith he still speaks, even though he is dead.

OFFERINGS

<u>PRAYER</u>

Father God, You set the offerings we are to give, so as
_____ commits his/her life to You, I ask You to
speak to him/her about the offerings You desire from
them. Direct him/her in all their giving. May there be an
outpouring of Your Spirit on them right now, that they will
hear clearly, hear correctly in what You are saying, Lord.
Bless their obedience; bless their offerings with an
abundant harvest they cannot contain. There will be no
lack in this house. There will be no disobedience in this
house. There will be no fear in this house, Lord. I
decree _____ is so blessed he/she will joyfully give
every time he/she hears Your voice. Cause him/her to
remember that it is You who gives them power to get
wealth so pour out that power right now, Father. He/she
will freely give what he/she has freely received from You
and their giving will be an act of worship unto You, Lord.
Blessed be the most high God who has delivered
_____ from all his/her enemies and enabled him/her
this day to freely give as Your Spirit directs. Thank You
for the power to give, Lord. In Jesus' mighty Name, we
pray, Amen.

SEED

SCRIPTURES
OLD TESTAMENT:

Amos 9:13

The days are coming, declares the Lord, when the reaper will be overtaken by the plowman and the planter by the one treading grapes. New wine will drip from the mountains and flow from all the hills.

Isaiah 55:9-11

As the heavens are higher than the earth, so are My ways higher than your ways and My thoughts than your thoughts. As the rain and the snow come down from heaven, and do not return to it without watering the earth and making it bud and flourish, so that it yields seed for the sower and bread for the eater, so is My Word that goes out from my mouth: It will not return to Me empty, but will accomplish what I desire and achieve the purpose for which I sent it.

SEED

<u>SCRIPTURES</u>
NEW TESTAMENT:

Mark 4:26-29

He also said, This is what the kingdom of God is like. A man scatters seed on the ground. Night and day, whether he sleeps or gets up, the seed sprouts and grows, though he does not know how. All by itself the soil produces grain—first the stalk, then the head, then the full kernel in the head. As soon as the grain is ripe, he puts the sickle to it, because the harvest has come.

2 Corinthians 9:6-7

Remember this: Whoever sows sparingly will also reap sparingly, and whoever sows generously will also reap generously. Each man should give what he has decided in his heart to give, not reluctantly or under compulsion, for God loves a cheerful giver.

SEED

<u>PRAYER</u>

Dear Father God, thank You for giving us Seeds to sow, and for teaching us that whatever we desire in our heart, we can give. I come to You now in agreement for _____ and the needs that he/she has. I thank You Father God that he/she can sow into the glory because they have been faithful with the tithes. Open up the heavens now God, so that there won't be room enough to contain the blessings and harvest for _____. You supply Seed to the sower and bread for food and You will also supply and increase the store of Seed and will enlarge the harvest of our righteousness. I pray for liberty for _____, for where the Spirit of the Lord is there is liberty. He/she is free to sow Seeds into the soil for the harvest that is desired. Thank You for that freedom and the faith that is springing up even now, Lord. So God gives him/her the opportunity and by Your wisdom he/she will know the soil to sow into. You are able to make all grace abound to _____ so that in all things and at all times having all that he/she needs, he/she will abound in every good work. Thank You for freedom to sow, in Jesus' Name, Amen.

MULTIPLICATION OF MONEY

SCRIPTURES
OLD TESTAMENT:

2 Kings 4:42-44

A man came from Baal Shalishah, bringing the man of God twenty loaves of barley bread baked from the first ripe grain, along with some heads of new grain. "Give it to the people to eat," Elisha said. "How can I set this before a hundred men?" his servant asked. But Elisha answered, "Give it to the people to eat. For this is what the Lord says: 'They will eat and have some left over.' " Then he set it before them, and they ate and had some left over, according to the word of the Lord.

Other Scripture:
1 Kings 17:7-15

MULTIPLICATION OF MONEY

SCRIPTURES
NEW TESTAMENT:

Luke 9:12-17

Late in the afternoon the Twelve came to him and said, "Send the crowd away so they can go to the surrounding villages and countryside and find food and lodging, because we are in a remote place here." He replied, "You give them something to eat." They answered, "We have only five loaves of bread and two fish—unless we go and buy food for all this crowd." (About five thousand men were there.) But he said to his disciples, "Have them sit down in groups of about fifty each." The disciples did so, and everybody sat down. Taking the five loaves and the two fish and looking up to heaven, he gave thanks and broke them. Then he gave them to the disciples to set before the people. They all ate and were satisfied, and the disciples picked up twelve basketfuls of broken pieces that were left over.

FINANCIAL PRESSURE

<u>SCRIPTURES</u>
OLD TESTAMENT:

Deuteronomy 8:18
But remember the Lord your God, for it is He who gives you the ability to produce wealth, and so confirms His covenant, which He swore to your forefathers, as it is today.

Malachi 3:10
Bring the whole tithe into the storehouse, that there may be food in My house. Test Me in this, says the Lord Almighty, and see if I will not throw open the floodgates of heaven and pour out so much blessing that you will not have room enough for it.

FINANCIAL PRESSURE

<u>SCRIPTURES</u>
NEW TESTAMENT:

2 Corinthians 8:14
At the present time your plenty will supply what they need, so that in turn their plenty will supply what you need. Then there will be equality.

Luke 6:38
Give, and it will be given to you. A good measure, pressed down, shaken together and running over, will be poured into your lap. For with the measure you use, it will be measured to you.

Hebrews 4:16
Let us then approach the throne of grace with confidence, so that we may receive mercy and find grace to help us in our time of need.

FINANCIAL PRESSURE

<u>PRAYER</u>

Dear Lord Jesus, I come to You and lift up _____ for the prayer of agreement. I ask You to remove the burden, and the financial pressure that he/she has been carrying. I thank You for setting the captive free, by Your blood. You said You want us to prosper as our soul prospers, so I come against anything that is hindering or preventing _____ from receiving Your blessings of prosperity. I call down more than enough. Remove fear, discouragement, pressure and guilt from their life, Lord. Send Your freedom and Your faith to him/her right now in immeasurable, overflowing waves of joy. Send down blessings and favor from heaven, Lord to encourage them that You are mindful of all they have been through. Unleash the power of Your Holy Spirit to deliver them from the burden over their finances. I thank You that You hear us when we pray and are faithful to answer when we call. I thank You for _____'s freedom today and giving him/her an anticipation of Your provision that is on the way. We expect a turnaround, a harvest of finances and every need met in the mighty Name of Jesus, Amen.

FINANCIAL MIRACLES

SCRIPTURES
OLD TESTAMENT:

Deuteronomy 8:18
But remember the Lord your God, for it is He who gives you the ability to produce wealth, and so confirms His covenant, which He swore to your forefathers, as it is today.

Malachi 3:10
Bring the whole tithe into the storehouse, that there may be food in My house. Test Me in this, says the Lord Almighty, and see if I will not throw open the floodgates of heaven and pour out so much blessing that you will not have room enough for it.

FINANCIAL MIRACLES

<u>SCRIPTURES</u>
NEW TESTAMENT:

2 Corinthians 8:14

At the present time your plenty will supply what they need, so that in turn their plenty will supply what you need. Then there will be equality.

Luke 6:38

Give, and it will be given to you. A good measure, pressed down, shaken together and running over, will be poured into your lap. For with the measure you use, it will be measured to you.

Hebrews 4:16

Let us then approach the throne of grace with confidence, so that we may receive mercy and find grace to help us in our time of need.

THE CHURCH

"In Christ we who are many form one body, and each member belongs to all the others."

Romans 12:5

THE LOCAL CHURCH

SCRIPTURES
OLD TESTAMENT:

Psalms 27:4
One thing I ask of the Lord, this is what I seek: that I may dwell in the house of the Lord all the days of my life, to gaze upon the beauty of the Lord and to seek him in his temple.

Psalms 149:1
Praise the Lord. Sing to the Lord a new song, His praise in the assembly of the saints.

THE LOCAL CHURCH

<u>SCRIPTURES</u>
NEW TESTAMENT:

Ephesians 1:23
Which is His body, the fullness of him who fills everything in every way.

1 Timothy 3:13
If I am delayed, you will know how people ought to conduct themselves in God's household, which is the church of the living God, the pillar and foundation of the truth.

Hebrews 10:25
Let us not give up meeting together, as some are in the habit of doing, but let us encourage one another—and all the more as you see the Day approaching.

THE LOCAL CHURCH

<u>PRAYER</u>

Lord, we pray today for _____. Pour out Your glory on this church, Holy Spirit. Lord, You said that the gates of hell would not prevail against Your Church so I ask that all the powers of darkness, offense, confusion, control in this church be destroyed now in Jesus' Name. Empower this church by Your Spirit to preach Your Word, to move in the spiritual gifts, and be free to receive unlimited measures of Your glory. Bless the pastors and leaders with supernatural wisdom and discernment and keep them in the center of their expertise, not swayed or moved by man but by Your Spirit. Cause these pastors, elders and leaders to speak the truth in love, and grow in grace as they are strengthened by the power of Your unconditional love. Help them to walk worthy of their calling by pleasing You and being fruitful in all their endeavors. Release Your glory, righteousness, peace and joy into their lives in abundance. Release overflowing finances to them, Father and make them good stewards of what You have given them. We pray in Jesus' mighty Name, Amen.

SOULS HARVEST

<u>SCRIPTURES</u>

Matthew 9:37-38
Then he said to his disciples, "The harvest is plentiful but the workers are few. Ask the Lord of the harvest, therefore, to send out workers into his harvest field."

Luke 10:2
He told them, "The harvest is plentiful, but the workers are few. Ask the Lord of the harvest, therefore, to send out workers into his harvest field."

SOULS HARVEST

<u>SCRIPTURES</u>

John 4:35

Do you not say, 'Four months more and then the harvest'? I tell you, open your eyes and look at the fields! They are ripe for harvest.

1 Corinthians 3:6-9

I planted the seed, Apollos watered it, but God made it grow. So neither he who plants nor he who waters is anything, but only God, who makes things grow. The man who plants and the man who waters have one purpose, and each will be rewarded according to his own labor. For we are God's fellow workers; you are God's field, God's building.

REVIVAL IN THE CHURCH

<u>SCRIPTURES</u>
OLD TESTAMENT:

Psalms 85:6-7
Will you not revive us again, that Your people may rejoice in You? Show us Your unfailing love, O Lord, and grant us Your salvation.

Habakkuk 2:14
The earth will be filled with the knowledge of the glory of the Lord, as the waters cover the sea.

REVIVAL IN THE CHURCH

<u>SCRIPTURES</u>
NEW TESTAMENT:

Matthew 5:14
You are the light of the world. A city on a hill cannot be hidden.

Acts 9:31
Then the church throughout Judea, Galilee and Samaria enjoyed a time of peace. It was strengthened and encouraged by the Holy Spirit; it grew in numbers, living in the fear of the Lord.

Matthew 16:18
And I tell you that you are Peter and on this rock I will build My Church, and the gates of Hades will not overcome it.

REVIVAL IN THE CHURCH

<u>PRAYER</u>

Father, in the mighty name of Jesus, I pray with _____ for a powerful revival in _____ Church. We lift You up in the midst of this congregation and exalt the beauty of Your holiness.

We thank You for pouring out Your glory Father, in unlimited measures, an outpouring and waves of Your Spirit.

Strengthen this church family with a wave of holiness and a fear of You, God. Pour out Your abundant mercy and grace on this church, Lord, that Your people would repent, turn back to You, seek Your presence and worship You in Spirit and in Truth.

Thank you for allowing revival to begin in the hearts of Your people, Lord. Revive the leaders and pastors with a fresh infilling of Your Spirit. Help them to be humble and broken before You and revive their hearts and minds with fresh fire from heaven. We pray in Jesus' mighty Name, Amen.

*"I am a Revival.
I am a Dispensation.
I am a Move – Because
in Him I live and move
and have my being!"*

Joshua Mills

PROMISES

*For no matter how many promises God has made,
they are "Yes" in Christ. And so through him the
"Amen" is spoken by us to the glory of God.*

2 Corinthians 1:20

PROMISES OF ANSWERED PRAYER

SCRIPTURES
OLD TESTAMENT:

Genesis 20:17
Then Abraham prayed to God, and God healed Abimelech, his wife and his slave girls so they could have children again.

1 Chronicles 4:10
Jabez cried out to the God of Israel, Oh, that You would bless me and enlarge my territory! Let Your hand be with me, and keep me from harm so that I will be free from pain. And God granted his request.

2 Chronicles 6:15
You have kept Your promise to Your servant David my father; with Your mouth You have promised and with Your hand You have fulfilled it—as it is today.

PROMISES OF ANSWERED PRAYER

<u>SCRIPTURES</u>
NEW TESTAMENT:

Luke 1:13
But the angel said to him: Do not be afraid, Zechariah; your prayer has been heard. Your wife Elizabeth will bear you a son, and you are to give him the name John.

Matthew 6:6
But when you pray, go into your room, close the door and pray to your Father, who is unseen. Then your Father, who sees what is done in secret, will reward you.

PROMISES OF ANSWERED PRAYER

PRAYER

Father God, You hear our prayers when we pray and we can have confidence in knowing that the answer is in You. I come into agreement with _____ for the answers he/she is waiting for. You are a God of truth and faithfulness, You are never late and Your timing is perfect. When we don't know what to do, we can cast our cares upon You and rest in Your arms knowing that You are moving on our circumstances with Your Spirit. Your Word is filled with precious promises and I ask You to quicken the Word to _____ as he/she meditates on those promises. Your Word will not return unto You void but it will accomplish all Your purposes. In Your presence is fullness of joy and pleasures forevermore so we seek Your face, Lord and trust You in all our ways. We worship You as we wait upon You with faith, patience and trust. There is none like You, Lord, Your mercies are new every morning. Fill us with new hope and joy that the answers for _____ are here because nothing is impossible with You; in Jesus' precious Name, Amen.

SEVEN PROMISES OF GOD

1. **He has promised to supply every need we have.** (Phillipians 4:19).

2. **God has promised that His grace is sufficient for us** (II Corinthians 12:9; Ephesians 2:8; Romans 5:2).

3. **God has promised that His children will not be overtaken with temptation** (I Corinthians 10:13; Jude 1:24; Daniel 6:16).

4. **God has promised us victory over death.** (Acts 2:32; I Corinthians 15:3,4; I Corinthians 15:57).

5. **God has promised that all things work together for good to those who love and serve Him faithfully** (Romans 8:28).

6. **God has promised that those who believe in Jesus and are baptized for the forgiveness of sins will be saved.** (Mark 16:16 and Acts 2:38).

7. **God has promised His people eternal life** (John 10:27,28).